For my mother and father

and for Patti Pate, the love of my life

Gender and Politics in Greek Tragedy

Artists and Issues in the Theatre

August W. Staub
General Editor

Vol. 7

PETER LANG
New York · Washington, D.C./Baltimore · Boston
Bern · Frankfurt am Main · Berlin · Vienna · Paris

Michael X. Zelenak

Gender and Politics in Greek Tragedy

PETER LANG
New York · Washington, D.C./Baltimore · Boston
Bern · Frankfurt am Main · Berlin · Vienna · Paris

Library of Congress Cataloging-in-Publication Data

Zelenak, Michael X.
Gender and politics in Greek tragedy / Michael X. Zelenak.
p. cm. — (Artists and issues in the theatre; vol. 7)
Includes bibliographical references.
1. Greek drama (Tragedy)—History and criticism. 2. Political plays, Greek—History and criticism. 3. Politics and literature—Greece. 4. Literature and society—Greece. 5. Gender identity in literature. 6. Women and literature—Greece. 7. Sex role in literature. I. Title. II. Series.
PA3136.Z44   882'.01—dc21   98-10448
ISBN 0-8204-4060-4
ISSN 1051-9718

Die Deutsche Bibliothek-CIP-Einheitsaufnahme

Zelenak, Michael X.:
Gender and politics in Greek tragedy / Michael X. Zelenak.
–New York; Washington, D.C./Baltimore; Boston; Bern;
Frankfurt am Main; Berlin; Vienna; Paris: Lang.
(Artists and issues in the theatre; Vol. 7)
ISBN 0-8204-4060-4

© 1998, 2005 Peter Lang Publishing, Inc., New York
275 Seventh Avenue, 28th Floor, New York, NY 10001
www.peterlangusa.com

All rights reserved.
Reprint or reproduction, even partially, in all forms such as microfilm, xerography, microfiche, microcard, and offset strictly prohibited.

Contents

Acknowledgments ix

Introduction 1

Chapter One
Tragedy and Politics: The Art Form of the Democracy 3

Chapter Two
Tragedy and Gender: Inventing the Female 17

Chapter Three
Tragedy and Pornography: Transvestite Ritual Theatre 33

Chapter Four
"Heifers Trapped by Wolves": Aeschylus' *Suppliant Maidens* 45

Chapter Five
"Not of Woman Born": The *Oresteia* 59

Chapter Six
A Woman's Place Is in the Tomb: Sophocles' *Antigone* 73

Chapter Seven
"The Best of All Possible Wives": Euripides' *Alcestis* 87

Chapter Eight
Euripides' Everywoman: *Medea* and the Dramaturgy of Gender 99

Chapter Nine
Resignation, Despair & the Great Capitulation: Sophocles' *Philoctetes* . 111

Chapter Ten
Death Throes of the Patriarchy: Euripides' Final Plays 123

Bibliography
A Guide to Further Reading 141

Index 151

Acknowledgments

I would like to thank Leon Katz, who inspired me to write this work, as well as Rolf Fjelde for his world-historical imagination, Richard Gilman for helping to shape and fine-tune my critical style in Yale's writing workshop, and Joel Schechter, who suggested this book to me.

I also wish to thank my comrades-in-arms and those who have shared or encouraged my work, including Earle Gister, Lloyd Richards, Rick Davis, Mel Shapiro, Brian Johnston, Gil Lazier, Stanley Kauffmann, Travis Preston, Chris Barreca, Steve Strawbridge, Catherine Zuber, JoAnne Akalaitis, Rick Grove, Julie Thompson, Geoff Cohen, Ceci Sommers, Virginia Manion, Gordon Rogoff, Jill Dolan, Don Marinelli, Chris Rawson, Anna Theresa Cascio, Larry Kornfeld, Lisa Humbertson, Norman Rhodes, Walter Bilderback, Jennifer Tipton, Pam Jordan, Ben Sammler, Mark Watts, David Coogle, Frank Trezza and John J. White.

I also owe a great debt to those who taught me Greek at the Bishop's Latin School—Rev. J. Berchmans Lanahan, S.J. and Rev. Joseph E. Henry, S.J.—and to Dr. Edwin Floyd at the University of Pittsburgh who helped me continue my studies in classics.

Finally, I wish to thank my students at Carnegie-Mellon, Yale, and especially Florida State for continuing to inspire and challenge me. I also wish to acknowledge the editing of Nancy Bell, the assistance of Peter Lang production manager Lisa Dillon, production assistant Karla Austin and acquisitions editor Owen Lancer, and especially the excellent comments and suggestions of series editor August Staub.

MXZ

Introduction

> The Greeks of the Periclean age were widely different from us. It is to be lamented that... there is no book which shows the Greeks precisely as they were; they seem all written for children, with the caution that no practice or sentiment, highly inconsistent with our own present manners, should be mentioned, lest these manners should receive outrage and violation.
>
> Percy Bysshe Shelley, "A Discourse on the Manners of the Ancients"

From my first encounters with Greek tragedy as a sixteen-year-old student at the all-male Bishop's Latin School in Pittsburgh, I was puzzled to learn that roles like Medea were originally played not by women but by men. When I questioned my teachers about this, I was told that this was "how things were." They added that this was not especially significant because most important institutions were still all male.

As I continued to study and teach the Greek plays over the next three decades, I found that more and more of what I saw in them was being passed over or ignored in the reverential mist that continues to keep them distant from most readers and enthusiasts of drama and theatre.

This book is my attempt to recover some of the immediacy which I believe the original audiences experienced. Aeschylus, Sophocles and Euripides were not writing timeless masterpieces but contemporary and imaginative readings of their culture and the events and problems confronting it. That the issues their plays confronted twenty-five centuries ago still spark debate, interest and even controversy is testimony to how unflinchingly honest they were in their examination and questioning.

Greek tragedy was born of and never wholly left the context of Athenian politics. As democracy emerged in Athens, tragedy and democracy became inextricably interwoven. Also interwoven with both tragedy and democracy was the concept and practice of patriarchy. Fifth-century Athens was rigidly masculine in its values and gender ideology.

The great festival of tragedy, the City Dionysia, with its many phallic features publicly celebrated the maleness of Athens. Tragedy had originated as an all-male event, a male-bonding ritual, and thus the earliest tragedies contained only male characters. Phrynichus changed the entire course of the history of tragedy by introducing female characters that, in the context of the all-male event, were naturally impersonated by male actors in drag. The transvestite portrayals of these new hyperfeminine creations quickly became popular.

The first three chapters explore historical features of politics and gender in fifth-century BC Athens as they relate to the institution of tragedy and the City Dionysia, sometimes by necessity in specific and somewhat specialized detail. The next seven chapters offer critical readings of particular plays by each of the three great tragedians examined in the light of the themes of gender and politics.

This book is addressed to the general audience of those interested in drama and theatre—not to Greek specialists or classicists. I have made every effort to make this work accessible to the non-Greek reader. All quotes in Greek are transliterated into the English alphabet. For the most part, I have used published translations for my citations from the texts, taking into account both readability and fidelity.

Had Athens produced nothing else but plays in the fifth century, it would still be one of the most remarkable cultural achievements in the western humanist tradition, which it helped create. Whatever comments or thoughts I have about these writers and their works I hope are accepted in the spirit of provoking further thought, inquiry, study and live production.

Michael X. Zelenak
Tallahassee, Florida
March 1998

Chapter One

Tragedy and Politics:
The Art Form of the Democracy

> You have never fully understood what sort of men these Athenians are.
> . . and how totally different they are from you. Above all they are
> innovators, quick with ideas and ways to put them into action . . . in
> politics, as in the arts, the new always prevails over the old.[1]
> Thucydides, 1.70–71

Greek tragedy was created under a very unique set of circumstances. To be precise, classical Greek tragedy was not actually "Greek" at all but was specifically and peculiarly Athenian, produced by and for the citizens of Athens alone. Any attempt to understand Greek tragedy should begin with an examination of its essential and primary motives, which were not literary or aesthetic but social and political.

Greek tragedies were, first and foremost, contemporary and immediate civic spectacle-events, a central feature of the cultural and political discourse of Athenian life. Aristotle identified this political aspect as a distinctive feature of fifth-century Greek tragedy when he said: "The earlier poets [i.e. Aeschylus, Sophocles, Euripides] made their characters talk 'politically' [*politikos*], the present-day poets rhetorically."[2] Greek tragedy was by its nature topical and contemporary, and the three major tragedians each examined the great social and political questions of their time.

The moment of Greek tragedy, as Jean-Pierre Vernant puts its, can be "very precisely defined in terms of time and space." He continues:

> It is born, flourishes, and disappears in Athens within the space of a hundred years. By the time Aristotle writes his *Poetics* the mainspring of tragedy is already broken for both the public and those writing for the theatre.[3]

Once Greek tragedy lost its hold on the Athenian imagination, it never regained it. By the mid-fourth century, revivals of "classic" tragedies were more significant than new productions, and the award for best actor had replaced that of best playwright as the most prestigious honor.

Athenian tragedy reached its cultural ascendency at the precise time that Athenian democratic ideology and political power reached their ascendancy in the Greek world. The Athenians were equally proud of their two greatest innovations—their unique civic festivals where plays were produced and their radical political system. In many ways, the citizens of Athens viewed these two native institutions—tragedy and democracy—as analogous. No distinction was made between the major civic liturgies required of wealthy citizens—the fitting of a trireme warship or a hoplite phalanx military unit to defend the city or the production of plays at one of the major dramatic festivals. Likewise, the average Athenian citizen was required to serve either in a hoplite phalanx or on a trireme or to perform in a tragic chorus, a prestigious civic-political duty which carried with it exemption from military service. Actors were paid directly by the state and were also eligible for deferment from military service.[4]

The founding and the major reorganizations of the dramatic festivals in Athens occurred at turning points in Athenian political life. Peisistratus the tyrant established the City Dionysia in 534 BC shortly after he secured absolute power (536 BC). Cleisthenes' new democratic constitution (508 BC), following the expulsion of the tyrants and the *coup* by democratic revolutionaries (510 BC), included major reforms in the City Dionysia. This initial decade of the democracy was a key transitional moment for tragedy and the City Dionysia. Major changes included the introduction of female characters, the inauguration of trilogies, the addition of the men's dithyrambic chorus, and a rebuilding of the Theatre of Dionysus.

Sixty years later, in the middle of the fifth century, Pericles altered both the political structure and the system of theatre production. This included the addition of another dramatic festival—the Lenaea, devoted primarily to comedy—and further renovation of the Theatre of Dionysus. Pericles also established the Theoric Fund—payment for attending plays—further reinforcing the civic nature of theatre. Citizens now received payment for all important public duties—service in the law courts, jury duty, attending meetings of the council and attendance at the theatre.

Democracy, like drama, is one of Athens' great legacies to western civilization. But just as we should not equate the conditions or purposes of Athenian drama with the modern theatre, it is equally important that we not confuse Athenian democracy with twentieth-century western democracy. Democracy in the fifth century BC was a dangerous and radical experiment. The concept of democracy supposedly had been introduced by the philosopher Pythagoras about 530 BC[5] and was promulgated by disciplined secret sects and underground political societies. Cleisthenes, Themistocles, Ephialtes, Pericles, and Cleon—whatever else they may have been—were radical revolutionaries whose very names inspired fear in conservative political circles throughout the Greek-speaking world and even beyond.

Democracy means "people power," or "masses power"—government by the many, the *dēmos*, instead of the few, that is the wealthy oligarchs (oligarchy) or well-born aristocrats (aristocracy). Democracy empowered a new ruling class, one that was expanded from a few hundred members of the wealthy elite families to the many thousands of native-born Athenian male citizens. The democrats never considered enfranchising women, metics (resident aliens), or slaves—at least three-quarters of the population was permanently excluded from the rights of citizenship. Furthermore, as Athenian democracy evolved in the fifth century, it did not move toward wider enfranchisement but rather imposed greater restrictions on citizenship.

The three-decade Peloponnesian War (431–404 BC) which ended Athenian political hegemony was a struggle to the death between two political ideologies: the conservative oligarchy (rule by the wealthy few) of Sparta, supported by tyrants (nonhereditary rulers) in other cities, and the revolutionary democracy (rule by the many) in Athens. Allegiances through the entire Greek world were determined by ideology. A change in government from oligarchy or tyranny to democracy in any city usually meant changing allegiances in the war. Both the Athenians and Spartans, through an intricate network of ambassadors-agents (*proxenoi*), tried to undermine governments, spread propaganda, arm insurgents and finance rebels. The Athenians understood that defeat meant not only economic and territorial loss but the end of their political system. Perhaps this explains some of Athens' more brutal actions during the war.

Tragedy had preceded democracy in Athens. The most important innovation in the history of tragedy—the introduction of "female masks" or "female characters"[6] by Phrynichus—occurred in the earliest years of the democracy. Changes in the floor plan and stage space also occurred before the end of the century. It is important to note that during the entire classical era both actors and chorus used the same space, the circular orchestra,[7] a democratic stage-space roughly equivalent to the American open-stage or the British arena-stage.

Athenian political ideology altered not only theatre practice but also theology. The god Dionysus underwent a major transformation in the early years of the democracy. In short, the effeminate, drunken, reveling god we are familiar with did not emerge until after the establishment of the Athenian democracy. Catherine Johns explains:

> Representations of Dionysus himself in early vase-paintings scarcely convey the impression of a wild and orgiastic fertility deity. Even though his influence over the vine and other growing things clearly mark him as a fertility god, he is not himself depicted as ithyphallic, except very occasionally in the form of a herm. On black figure pottery [530–500 BC] he is shown as a dignified, bearded god wearing a long robe and crowned with vine leaves, retaining a solemn and restrained bearing however wild the cavorting of the followers who surround him.[8]

Dionysus was not an urban god but a rural deity, and his incorporation by Peisistratus as the patron deity of a major new civic festival was probably part of a conscious political policy to unify Attica. Later, the democracy's ability to consolidate power and create a unified central government for all of Attica helps to explain Athens' rapid rise to political and economic prominence. Dionysus, a popular rural deity and patron of the country revels known as the Rural Dionysia, was the glue that cemented the city and the country districts into the city-state of Athens/Attica.

> When Peisistratus brought Dionysus into prominence and made tragedy the main attraction of this festival, he was honoring a newcomer in the Olympic pantheon—a god not so much of the old aristocracy as of the common folk, who had worshiped him with rejoicings in their villages.[9]

Thespis was likely involved with local cults of Dionysus in his rural home district of Icaria before he brought tragedy to Athens.

Dionysus' transformation from a dignified masculine godhead to the transvestite (or feminized) reveler was part of a comprehensive gender-related political agenda. Male godheads usurped numerous functions of female deities during the archaic era as the vestiges of the matrilinear Minoan culture were displaced. The metamorphosis of Dionysus reflects changes in gender ideology emerging in Athens during the sixth century. For example, as George Thomson notes, the original *thiasos* (sacred band of revelers) of Dionysus were all female[10]—a male priest leading a band of female followers, such as maenads. However, by the early democratic era, the Dionysian worshipers/revelers began to be represented as primarily male satyrs—often sporting long phalluses. Likewise, the great Mysteries of Eleusis were initially an exclusively female ritual organized around the goddess Demeter. By the sixth century, Dionysus had became an integral and coequal part of the mysteries, which were no longer open only to women.

Dionysus was not only a rural deity; he had great appeal to the urban masses. E. R. Dodds explains:

> Dionysus is a democratic god: he is accessible to all, not like the Pythian Apollo, through priestly intermediaries, but directly in his gift of wine and through membership of his *thiasos*. His worship probably made its original appeal mainly to people who had no citizenship rights in the "gentle state" and were excluded from the older cults associated with the great families.[11]

Anyone, rich or poor, had quick and easy access to the Dionysian godhead.

The new Dionysian festival "furthered Peisistratus' policy of directing the religious loyalties of the people toward the *polis* and himself and away from the hereditary cults of aristocratic families."[12] As François de Polignac points out, "Religious rituals guaranteed a mutual recognition of statuses and set the seal upon membership of the society, thereby defining an early form of citizenship."[13] The civic function of the religious cults should not be overlooked. The theatre and its Dionysian rituals became the central Athenian secular civic ritual.

With the new democratized Dionysus as patron deity, tragedy quickly became the main vehicle for the promulgation of civic propaganda and the new democratic ideology in Athens. Because of the success and popularity of these unique spectacle-festivals, democracy became entrenched there. The City Dionysia became the major civic and patriotic event of the year for Athenian citizens. Plays were not entertainments for a special audience of theatregoers but public festivals lavishly funded by the state and attended by the entire citizen body. All normal public and private business of the *polis* was suspended; the law courts were closed as was the *agora* (marketplace).

The City Dionysia holiday included not only plays but also other civic, military and religious spectacles. Prominently seated in places of honor were the priest(s) of Dionysus and the ten popularly elected generals, who presided at the opening ceremonies. A highlight of the festival was the parade of the ephebes, the young military cadets about to enter active military service. Often, speeches honoring war heroes or those who had prominently served the state also were included as were ceremonies inducting into military service the sons of Athenian citizens who had fallen in battle. Theatre celebrated the *dēmos*, the masses, and the democratic state. Like the *ekklēsia* (assembly), it was presented in the open air before the entire citizenry. Just as the members of the *boulē* (council) were selected from each of the ten tribes to make major executive political decisions, the victors at tragic competitions were chosen by a representative from each tribe. In short, tragedy was the art form of the democracy.

Tragedy in the fifth century never became an independent aesthetic form that developed solely on its own terms. It always retained key elements of civic ritual and political propaganda. Changes in the formal structure or physical requirements of tragedy were not merely artistic choices but official civic and legal responsibilities. Only a handful of such changes were ever made.

With the establishment of the radical democracy, tragedy became the official state-sponsored spectacle to celebrate the greatness of Athens' political and social system. The one thousand drachma fine on Phrynichus for his *Sack of Miletus* (492 BC),[14] which criticized Athenian political policy, indicates that tragedy was not intended to question or challenge government policy and official ideology. Conversely, the propagandistic celebration of the Athenian state and its democratic values was obviously encouraged. Theatre and politics remained intertwined. Themistocles, as *chorēgos*, used the production of Phrynichus' *Phoenicians* to attempt to strengthen his political power base just as Pericles later used the *Persians* to launch his own political career.

Theatre, society, politics and civic ideology in fifth-century Athens interacted in a complex symbiosis. In exploring the political and civic spectacle/discourse of Greek tragedy, we must be careful neither to reduce nor oversimplify. The relationship between social reality and mimetic representation is always problematic because theatre, as all art, indeed all discourse, "reflects" life not necessarily in direct or literal one-on-one correspondences, but often, if not usually, in contradictory and paradoxical ways. Even a journeyman playwright like Eugene Scribe understood this when he stated in his acceptance speech at the French Academy that the theatre was "not truth but fiction. The Theatre is therefore rarely the direct expression of social life. . . . It is often the inverse expression."[15] The fictive spectacle/discourse of Greek tragedy did not imitate reality, but rather it presented an imaginary structure of human experience.

A vexing problem in literary and cultural studies is caused by the fact that the ideas and beliefs most important to a culture are rarely explicitly stated. They are so obvious to those of their own time that they need not be articulated. Furthermore, the central values of a culture are not simply a group of ideas or fixed thoughts. Cultural values and shared ideology are a process and a series of strategies—they are what make things make sense, how contradictory ideas are able to cohere—what Raymond Williams termed a "structure of feelings."[16]

Greek tragedy staged spectacles of crime or transgression against a central ideological premise or institution of the Athenian *polis*. Plato questioned the civic usefulness of tragedy by asking how such events helped to produce good citizens. He argued that the staging of these transgressions in the emotionally charged environment of tragedy legitimized those actions and put dangerous and subversive models before the citizens. However, the conflicts and debates of tragedy did not occur within a threatening or subversive context; the environment was controlled and the debate shaped by its civic framework and the constraints of its heavily determined formal structure. The crimes of the heroes of tragedy did not legitimize transgression; quite the contrary, the spectacle of tragedy emotionally empowered democratic cultural values and legitimized the political and social order. Tragedy refined and expressed not dissident views but the dominant ideology of the Athenian *polis*. As Richard Seaford asserts, "In the extant tragedies (or tragic trilogies) the only *communities* that suffer disaster in the end are non-Greek."[17] Tragedy was a civic institution that celebrated the greatness of the *polis* and, in the process, reassured its citizen cocelebrants of its open-mindedness and fairness.

It is rather astonishing that no articulation or theoretical defense of democracy survives from Athens in the classical era, except perhaps obliquely in Pericles' famous funeral oration recorded by Thucydides. It seems as if none were ever written. Is it possible that democratic Athens created no Patrick Henry, no Thomas Paine, no Danton, no Marx, no Trotsky, no Lenin? And inspired no *Rights of Man*, no *Manifesto of the Communist Party*, no *State and Revolution*? Nicole Loraux provides the answer with her observation that "the Athenian democracy scarcely had time to elaborate its own theory."[18] Democracy was an expediency, an ad hoc invention of Cleisthenes and his fellow revolutionaries who overthrew the tyranny and replaced it with a political system radically different from oligarchy. As Loraux puts it, democracy was "a polemical concept forged in the political battle against those supporters of oligarchy."[19] Democracy, in other words, became a practical political reality before its abstract ideals or theoretical principles ever existed. In the context of this intellectual-political vacuum, the new democratized civic ritual of tragedy rapidly became the major vehicle for the articulation of the principles and ideology of the democratic *polis* in fifth-century Athens.

Myth and other shared stories are essential to the creation of cultural and social values. Radical social and political changes challenge not only the political order and social institutions but the values and very meaning of a culture. To retell the known stories and reconfigure the traditional myths in order to "make sense" again is sociologically reassuring. The establishment of democracy in Athens challenged long-standing social structures and values. Tragedy explained the new civic ideology by staging the spectacle of values in transition alongside familiar icons of continuity. It is significant that tragedy, the central civic institution of the democratic *polis*, staged the struggles, not of ordinary citizens, but of heroic figures from the mythical past. All Greek myths were drawn from the nondemocratic heroic age, and the great heroes were, in reality, wealthy oligarches and tyrants from an earlier era, the very antithesis of the Athenian citizen-democrat. Tragedy became the vehicle to integrate and domesticate these heroic legends into the values of the Athenian democratic *polis*. Through tragedy, the city rewrote the myths of the heroic age and enlisted them into the service of the democratic ideology. As Justina Gregory explains: "It juxtaposes the characters of the legend with the world of the fifth-century *polis* in order to bring into focus the divergent values of the inherited culture and the new social order."[20]

Myth is neither timeless nor apolitical. The politics of mythology was a central part of Athenian civic discourse. Because Greek religion contained no sacred text, the entire body of myth was conveniently open to reinterpretation by each author, and audiences expected playwrights to come up with unique versions of the myths. Each tragedy staged a revision of a myth, and the Greek playwrights were as free with their myths as

Shakespeare was with English history. Greek tragedies were living civic books and history texts rewritten to show the continuity of the human experience and its world-historical culmination in the fifth-century Athenian *polis*. Each playwright freely adapted the myths to place them within the context of contemporary civic and political discourse. The extremity of the conflict and the apparent challenges to civic institutions might appear to be subversive, but the expropriation of the myths and their adaptation to the political discourse was a legitimization of the political system as well as a celebration of the Athenian *polis* and its citizens.

The system of meaning in the spectacle/discourse of Greek tragedy emerges from a dual perspective on its action, with the chorus usually representing the view of the contemporary Athenian citizen-democrat (audience) while the protagonist stands as an extreme type, often a representative of the values of an earlier era. Although the presence of the chorus stressed the communal aspects of the dramatic experience, we should not make the mistake of equating choral moralizing with the meaning of the play or the author's personal beliefs. The meaning of the play emerges from the interaction of the two perspectives: the heroically extreme and the appropriately moderate. Our intellect responds to the objective expression of wisdom and moderation, while our emotions are pulled toward the heroism and suffering of the extreme individualist. Furthermore, the chorus does not always represent the norm of moderation. In Aeschylus, for example, the choruses of *Seven Against Thebes*, *Suppliant Maidens* and *Eumenides* stake out radical and extreme postures. In some tragedies, there is no "norm" or moderate point of view expressed. What is termed Euripidean cynicism is largely due to his banishment of any normative perspective. Euripides presents the norm as a perversion or even a parody. The "normal" can then be reexamined and reperceived as grotesque, pathological or absurd.

The chorus, like the actor, is not a psychological entity but a specific set of functions that varied from play to play. For example, the chorus often provides a sympathetic perspective from which the extreme actions of the protagonist are mediated for the audience. Without the perspective of the chorus foregrounding Ajax, he would remain little more than a raving madman. Antigone would be a dangerous radical feminist without the mediating influence of the male chorus which deflects the action at crucial moments in the play and carefully controls the ideological discourse.

The chorus was not merely important to Greek tragedy. Without the chorus, drama could not take place. The performance space was set up not in reference to the actors but to the chorus (*orchestra*, "dancing place"); plays were called "dramatic choruses"; the term for playwright was not writer or poet but *didaskalos* (teacher), because he was the one who taught the chorus. What contemporary theatregoers or readers would assume to be the most important parts of a play—the scenes between the actors ("episodes")—were, formally, the things that came between and interrupted the choral sections. The chorus usually set the emotional tone and shaped the terms of debate of the tragedy, and it was often the communal spokesperson for Athenian democratic ideology. Just as their politics was shaped by the collective experience, so was their drama. Athenian tragedy and politics share the same ideological structure of experience. Democracy empowered both the individual and the community in a new way. Democracy and tragedy both sought to mediate the interests of the individual and the group. Just as the citizen had no significance without the community, the actor could not exist without the chorus.

As tragedy became more complex in its discourse, more sophisticated tactics were required to reinvent and restore the ideological balance. What Aeschylus could take for granted, Sophocles would have to struggle with his heroic artistry to reconfigure and sustain. The surviving Greek tragedies record a crisis of values that occurred during the latter part of the fifth century. The very deftness with which Sophocles and Euripides could manipulate ethical-moral debate, the fact that basic moral concepts could be used by different characters in the same play with opposite force, the cynicism and the emptying-out of morality in Euripides, is evidence of the extreme crisis of morality Athens was attempting to confront and exorcize.

The action of every tragedy begins with a conflict that threatens a civic institution or central ideological premise of the Athenian *polis*. It ends when this action is reversed and the conflict is solved or terminated, *and the ideological premise or threatened institution is restored or reconfigured*. Tragedy does not celebrate chaos but order; it does not legitimize civil disobedience but the unshakable institutions of the democratic *polis*.

The content of Greek tragedy often seems controversial, but it was not ideologically subversive. Tragedy was not simply a group of characters or a series of speeches and arguments but a system of dramatic action. The civic-dramatic festivals created a sacred space and time where the celebrants enacted a privileged discourse in the fictive but real realm of myth. Tragedy created conflicts, but it also controlled, mediated and resolved them. With both extreme emotional content and enormous formal constraints, tragedy was an analogue for the structure of human experience itself. Its interplay between actor and chorus also duplicated the model of civic and political discourse. Each tragedy presented an imaginative reading (or misreading) of the social text to its audience of citizens.

A number of plays by Euripides, with their ironic, mythical rewritings, antiheroes and cynical reversals, overtly question, if not attack, central ideological premises of the democratic *polis*. Clearly, these plays were controversial. Many citizens and some political leaders felt that playwrights like Euripides were going too far and abusing the dramatic license. During the Peloponnesian War, both Euripides and Aristophanes were brought to trial for treason in an attempt to reassert direct political control over the theatre just as an earlier generation had fined Phrynichus for the *Sack of Miletus*. However, Euripides' and Aristophanes' acquittals reinforced the right of theatre to address any issue without censorship, even at the City Dionysia, the great public celebration of Athenian power, attended by visitors and dignitaries from all over the Greek world.

Greek tragedy's transformation from political pageant and civic spectacle/discourse to dramatic art is one of the great miracles of western civilization. Its historical moment was brief. Our extant plays cover a period of less than seventy years, from 472 to 405 BC. Even at the time, fifth-century Athenians were not unaware of the significance of their drama. Throughout all the sufferings and hardships of the Peloponnesian

War, including the protracted sieges of Athens, internal strife, massive civil disobedience, economic collapse, a *coup d'état* and a counterrevolution, the city never canceled its drama festivals. In the closing days of the war, with Athens cut off and encircled by the Spartan armies, Aristophanes, in *Frogs*, exhorted his countrymen to rally and save the city—not in order to preserve the empire, not for the honor of their city, not to save their freedom, not even for her democracy, but so that Athens could continue to produce plays. Athens' greatest achievement, as Aristophanes knew, was not her military prowess nor her empire nor her fleet, nor even her unique political system, but her drama.

Notes

[1] Charles Forster Smith, trans., *History of the Peloponnesian War*, 4 vols. (Cambridge, Mass.: Harvard University Press, 1919–23). All translations of Thucydides are from this edition.

[2] Gerald F. Else, trans., *Poetics* (Ann Arbor: University of Michigan Press, 1967), p. 28. *Poetics*, 1450b.

[3] Jean-Pierre Vernant and Pierre Vidal-Nauqet, *Myth and Tragedy in Ancient Greece*, trans. Janet Lloyd (New York: Zone, 1990), p. 89.

[4] Arthur Pickard-Cambridge, *The Dramatic Festivals of Athens*, rev. J. Gould and D. M. Lewis, 2nd ed. (Oxford: Clarendon Press, 1988), p. 77.

[5] George Thomson, *Aeschylus and Athens: A Study in the Social Origins of Drama* (New York: Grosset and Dunlap, 1968), p. 210.

[6] The Suda, *Life of Phrynichus*, cited in A.E. Haigh, *The Tragic Drama of the Greeks* (Oxford: Clarendon Press, 1896), p. 45.

[7] Margarete Bieber, *The History of the Greek and Roman Theatre* (Princeton: Princeton University Press, 1939), p. 111.

[8] Catherine Johns, *Sex or Symbol: Erotic Images of Greece and Rome* (Austin: University of Texas Press, 1982), p. 81.

[9] Alan M. G. Little, *Myth and Society in Attic Drama*, rpt. of 1942 ed. (New York: Octagon, 1967), p. 22.

[10] Thomson, *Aeschylus and Athens*, p. 149.

[11] E. R. Dodds, ed., *Euripides' Bacchae*, 2nd ed. (Oxford: Clarendon Press, 1960), pp. 127–28.

[12] William Blake Tyrrell and Frieda S. Brown, *Athenian Myths and Institutions* (Oxford: Oxford University Press, 1991), p. 59.

[13] François de Polignac, *Cults, Territory, and the Origins of the Greek City-State*, trans. Janet Lloyd (Chicago: University of Chicago Press, 1995), p. 153.

[14] Herodotus, *The History*, 6.21.

[15] Stephen Stanton, ed., *Camille and Other Plays* (New York: Hill and Wang, 1957), p. xvii, note.

[16] Raymond Williams, *Drama from Ibsen to Brecht* (New York: Oxford University Press, 1969), p. 17.

[17] Richard Seaford, *Reciprocity and Ritual: Homer and Tragedy in the Developing City-State* (Oxford: Clarendon Press, 1994), p. xiv.

[18] Nicole Loraux, *The Invention of Athens: The Funeral Oration in the Classical City*, trans. Alan Sheridan (Cambridge, Mass.: Harvard University Press, 1986), p. 173.

[19] Loraux, *The Invention of Athens*, p. 174.

[20] Justina Gregory, *Euripides and the Instruction of the Athenians* (Ann Arbor: University of Michigan Press, 1991), p. 7.

Chapter Two

Tragedy and Gender: Inventing the Female

> For women are the biggest single bad thing Zeus
> has made for us; a ball-and-chain; we can't get loose.[1]
> Semonides of Amorgos, "An Essay on Women," 115–16

> Mistresses [*hetairas*] we keep for the sake of pleasure, concubines [*pallakas*] for the daily care of our persons, but wives [*gunaikas*] to bear us legitimate children and to be faithful guardians of our households.[2]
> Demosthenes, *Against Neaera*, 59.122

Gender is a function of politics, economics and sociology; sexuality is biological. Often the two overlap, and there is no consensus as to exactly where politics begins and biology ends. Sexuality can imperceptibly acquire attributes of gender, and gender is often hidden in supposedly neutral or nonsexual terrain—for example, language, religion and literature.

The production of plays in fifth-century Athens was a microcosm of the civic and political life, which meant, literally, that men wrote all the parts and acted all the roles. Theatre, like politics, was a sexually exclusive ritual. Its celebrants were all male. The only possible evidence we have that the audiences for tragedy in fifth-century Athens were not all male is a story in the ancient *Life of Aeschylus*: "Some say that during the performance of the *Eumenides*, when he brought the chorus on one by one, he so frightened the audience that children fainted and unborn infants were aborted."[3] It should be pointed out that this description was written several centuries after the event and that the ancient "lives of the poets" are often unreliable in specific details. Here, the general observation is well noted—that the chorus in the *Eumenides* was startling and brilliantly staged. Scholars seem unwilling to admit the fact that there is no solid evidence to support the widely accepted assumption that theatre audiences included women.[4] On the contrary, all indications point to the opposite conclusion—that tragedy was by its nature an exclusively male experience.

The privileged maleness of all Athenian social institutions, including theatre, is not an irrelevant feature that has no bearing on art or aesthetics. The fact that Greek theatre was an exclusively male ritual, requiring even transvestite male performers for the female roles, is a key aspect of the plays that were created and presented. It is astonishing that so little has been written about this highly unusual and extraordinary feature of Greek theatre. Would those who believe this information to be insignificant feel the same if archaeologists unearthed plays by the poet Sappho and discovered that they, and hundreds of other plays on the island of Lesbos, were written and produced exclusively by and for women with all the male roles played by women? Would this be ignored as a trivial and irrelevant quirk with little or no bearing on the meaning of the works?

The classical Greek biological understanding of sexuality was based upon opposition. By their natures, the female was opposed to the male, just as earth was opposed to heaven, fire to water. This is not unusual. Roger Just explains:

> In any society the concept of masculinity and femininity are defined by mutual opposition and women tend to be portrayed as what men, ideally, are not.[5]

The Greeks delighted in intellectual oppositions and the dialectical play of ideas, whether in tragedy, the law courts, symposia, the assembly or in philosophical essays cast as dramatic "dialogues," but, they also recognized two types of opposition. One spurred man to greater achievement, the other was destructive. Hesiod outlines this in the opening of *Works and Days*:

> Upon the earth
> Two strifes exist; the one is praised by those
> Who come to know her, and the other blamed.
> (12–14)[6]

Opposition between male and female was perceived as a central fact of life. Needless to say, it was a woman, Pandora, who introduced destructive sexual antagonism as well as "Lies and persuasive words and cunning ways" (line 78). Lying and the very concept of deception had been invented by a woman. Furthermore, the closest to a generic descriptive term for women, *genos gunaikōn* ("race of women"), implied that women were not merely a separate gender but a separate species.[7]

In fifth-century Athens, all aspects of sexuality were gender-determined, and, as can be expected, the ideology of gender replicated the social reality and justified the existing political order. The "male" meant the dominant, the "female" the subordinate; the male the active, the female the passive; the male rational, the female irrational; the male strong, the female weak; the male virtuous, the female immoral; the male honest, the female deceptive; the male brave, the female cowardly.

The gender ideology of Athens can be gleaned by opening any dictionary of Attic Greek and examining words descriptive of sexuality. For example, the adjective *thēlus*, "of female sex, of or belonging to women," means "womanish, weak, effeminate." Its verbal form, *thēluno*, means "to make weak and womanish." This single root, from the word *thēlē* ("the part of the breast which gives suck"), supplies us with a long list of compound forms, almost all of which have negative connotations if not denotations. Conversely, the equivalent adjective for "male" or "masculine," *arrēn*, means "manly, strong," and from it are formed the words *aretē*, "goodness, virtue" and *aristos*, "best, most excellent."[8] Similarly, in Latin, the word for "virtue," *virtus*, is derived from the word for "man," *vir*.

Classical Attic Greek did not possess a generic word for "woman" to correspond to *anēr*, "man." The word *gunē*, "wife" or "wife/woman," or the phrase *genos gunaikōn*, "race of wife/women," was routinely used in this capacity. *Anthrōpos* could be employed generically for "human being" as "man" is in English. But in a gender dominant society, the presumed universality of such concepts must be suspect. Although there was a host of words to distinguish the subtle shades of meaning between different types of "whore" and "prostitute," such as *pallaka, hetaira, pornē*, concepts such as "woman," or "unmarried woman" or "single woman" are notions that the classical Greeks could express only metaphorically or by implication. Attic philology is sociologically and politically precise in telling us that a "female" could be a mother (*mētēr*) or a daughter (*thugatēr*) or a sister (*adelphē*), a virgin (*parthenos*) or a whore (*pornē*), a wife (*gunē* or the archaic *damar*, literally "brought under the yoke") or a bride (*numphos*) but not simply a woman.

Male homosexuality likewise had to conform to gender precepts. To be male meant to be the dominant partner in the sex act—the male mounted, the female was penetrated, or "wife/women do not mount sexually but are mounted,"[9] as Aristotle put it. To the Greeks, for whom narrowly polarized concepts of homosexuality and heterosexuality had not yet developed, sexual attraction between men, especially that of older men for young boys, was considered natural, and society provided numerous outlets to gratify these desires. In many cities, both the military and educational systems encouraged or institutionalized sexual relations between older men and young boys. Sparta is the best known example. Love and sexual relationships in Greek tragedy were not always heterosexual. Many plays—all of them lost—dealt openly with homosexual love, such as Aeschylus' *Myrmidons*, which treated Achilles' passion for Patroclus, Sophocles' *Lovers* [*erastai*] *of Achilles*, and Euripides' *Chrysippus*, which explored homosexual incest. Some plays even explored aberrant sexuality such as bestiality (Aeschylus' *Cretan Women* and Euripides' *Cretans*).

Sexual acts between males, however, were socially acceptable only if they did not violate the precepts and expectations of gender. Children and slaves, in term of political and social status, were analogous to women; thus the sexual act between men was deemed acceptable only if the male citizen was the dominant "masculine" partner (*erastēs*) in the sexual act with a young boy or male slave as the passive "feminine" partner (*eromenos*).[10] If a male citizen allowed himself to be penetrated as the passive partner in anal sex, this "female" action was considered unnatural and reprehensible.

In the fourth century, in a much discussed passage, the orator Aeschines used this very charge to destroy one of his political opponents, Timarkhos, a friend and political ally of Demosthenes. Aeschines declared:

> And shall you let Timarkhos go free, a man charged with the most shameful conduct? This man who has committed a woman's offence with a male body. If so, how can any of you punish a woman whom you have found to have done wrong?[11]

Theatre was not unique in its exclusion of women. Tragedy was an important civic-political function, and it would have seemed natural to Athenian citizens that only men should participate since all other major Athenian civic and political institutions were exclusively male. Neither the word for citizen (*politēs*) nor the word for Athenian (*Athēnaios*) even had a feminine form.[12] Wives and daughters of citizens were denied education and segregated from the company of men. Women could not register in the *dēmoi* (districts) or *phratrai* (brotherhoods) as citizens, could not vote or attend the assembly, hold office, own or dispose of property or give testimony in court. If a woman's testimony was essential in the law court, it was handled exactly as it was in the theatre. A male, in this case the husband or guardian, after suitable rehearsal, was allowed to "speak for" the woman and enter her testimony—that is he read her lines and played her part—just as male actors impersonated women in the theatre.[13]

And yet, Athenian men seemed to give women in the drama what they denied them in real life—equal, if not top, status. Great female parts are one of the legacies of Greek tragedy. Arguably, the greatest character created by each of the three tragedians was female. *Philoctetes* alone among the thirty-two extant tragedies has no female characters.

Froma Zeitlin argues that female characters in Greek tragedy were needed to play the central role of the "radical other" to the male psyche:

> *Functionally* women are never an end in themselves, and nothing changes for them once they have lived out their drama onstage. Rather, they play the role of catalysts, agents, instruments, blockers, spoilers, destroyers, and sometimes helpers or saviors for the male characters. When elaborately represented, they may serve as antimodels as well as hidden models for the masculine self. . . .[14]

One means of controlling ideological discourse is the strategy of opposition. The two most common types of female characters in Greek tragedy—the passive, suffering "female" victim, such as Cassandra, Ismene and Alcestis, to name an example from each tragedian, and the active, destructive "male" woman, such as Clytemnestra, Antigone and Medea—are not portrayed as two of many possible types of female representation but as opposites, the two polar or archetypal extremes of female behavior. Sometimes, as in the *Agamemnon* and the *Antigone*, they are placed beside each other for contrast. A female character is presented as either one or the other, or she begins as one and ends as the other, as does Hecuba in the *Hecuba*. Furthermore, gender ideology is promulgated and reinforced not only by positive displays of the proper behavior in each sex but also by the negative exhibitions of extreme or improper models. Gender displacement, gender inversion and gender transgression are extremely important to Greek tragedy.

Linguistically, we think of the "best" as a superlative concept; for example, the person with the "most bravery" we would call the "bravest." Not so the Greeks. As Greek choruses never seem to weary of telling us, and as Aristotle explains in the *Nichomachean Ethics*, virtues cease to be virtues when they are taken to the extreme of either "too much" or "too little." The "best" of something is not the "most" but the "proper amount," neither too much nor too little. Thus, in virtues and attributes, the "best" is the "most moderate." A man who has too much bravery is foolhardy—this is the true meaning of *hubris*—while one who possesses too little is a coward. A truly brave man has exactly the right amount of bravery.

As with virtues, so with gender. The model female should fall between the two extremes; in real life, a woman should neither be too womanly nor not womanly enough. Conversely, with male characters, displays of nonmanly or "female" behavior, such as emotions, were a sign of weakness. Ajax is shamed as much by his confusion and irresolution (i.e. womanly feelings) as he is by his grotesque crimes:

> My mood, which just before was strong and rigid,
> No dipped sword more so, now has lost its edge—
> My speech is womanish for this woman's sake
> And pity touches me for my wife and child.
>   (650–53)[15]

The paragon of manliness and misogyny, Herakles, is humiliated when his overwhelming pain drives him to tears and the expression of emotion: "Now in my misery I am discovered a woman" (*Women of Trachis*, 1075).[16] Aeschylus' Aegisthus is the archetype of the "womanly man"; he is referred to by the chorus as "*gunē*" (wife/woman).

Gender ideology proclaimed that women were by nature weak, irrational, ruled by passion and emotion, prone to deception and driven by sexual desire. Athenian physicians invented the term *husteria* or *hysteria* (from *hustera*, womb) to diagnose the mysterious but persistent disease that afflicted only women. Its womanly symptoms were excessive passion, irrationality, anorexia and a self-destructive depression.[17] Men, on the other hand, were by nature strong, logical, practical, honest and competitive. Although the "male virtues" were celebrated, maleness taken to extremes could be just as dangerous as femaleness taken to extremes. In the healthy social-sexual ideal, both men and women should be able to restrain their natural impulses, which were dangerous in the extreme, and attain the proper balance of "appropriate" genderization.

The male world was public, the woman's sphere was private. As Xenophon tells us, "The god, from the very beginning, designed the nature of women for the indoor work and concerns and the nature of man for the outdoor work" because men were given "a greater share of courage."[18] According to nature, men ruled and women obeyed. The Athenians did not view their patriarchal system as tyrannical or unjust—any more than later patriarchal cultures would—but rather as a middle road, a moderating influence upon what would have otherwise been unrestrained violence by men and uncontrollable irrationality by women. Without the civilizing graces of the Athenian patriarchy and androcentric constitution, society would fall into chaos or, even worse, potentially devolve into the ultimate nightmare—domination by women.

The myth of the Amazons and the war of liberation to free Athenian males from female domination—the *Amazonomachia*—led by the founding father of Athens, Theseus, is a central legitimizing myth of the Athenian *polis*. The Amazons were inverted males, savage women warriors who cut off their breasts (*amazos*, "no breast"), fought wars, pillaged cities and raped men indiscriminately. As the historian Diodorus of Sicily relates:

> Beside the river Thermodon, therefore, a nation ruled by females held sway, in which the women pursued the arts of war just like the men. They relate that one of these women who held the royal authority excelled in courage and physical strength; and having organized and trained an army of women, she subjugated some of the neighboring tribes. . . . she constantly undertook wars against the surrounding peoples; . . . To the men she relegated the spinning of wool and other household tasks of women. She promulgated laws whereby she led forth the women to martial strife, while on the men she fastened humiliation and servitude.[19]

Scenes from the *Amazonomachia* were prominently displayed on Athens' Parthenon. A political scandal was caused when it was discovered that Pericles had secretly bribed an artist to add "a particularly fine likeness of Pericles fighting an Amazon."[20] The artist was punished, but the incident seems not to have hurt Pericles' popularity—it may well have boosted it.

The Amazons are the paradigm of gender-inverted sexual stereotypes. They never existed. They were born not on the banks of the Thermodon River but in the imagination of Athenian males; they were not women but inverted males. They are related to the many other fantastic female monsters that fill Greek mythology, from Gorgons, Furies, Sirens and Harpies to Scylla and Charybdis. All versions of the female from the classical age were masculinized fictions. They were created for contemplation by men, and, in fact, they never purport to be anything more. The female, politically and artistically, was an invented category.

Athenians felt especially blessed not only because they had saved themselves and the rest of Greece from the bloodthirsty Amazonian hordes but also because they were *autochthonos* ("earth-born")—referring to the miraculous birth of Erichthonius, the founder of the city of Athens. The god

Hephaestus, while sexually pursuing the goddess Athena, inadvertently ejaculated sperm that fell upon the earth, landing on the site of the future city of Athens. From the fertile impregnated soil sprung Erichthonius, the founder and first king of Athens, from whom all Athenians claimed their descent. As Simon Goldhill points out:

> It is not by chance that the city which in practice relieved women of power, position, even the name of citizen, should in its mythic projection tell stories which either exclude women totally in even their function as child-producers, or, alternately... establish the race of women not only as separate from men but also as a race whose control or overthrow is necessary for the progress of civilization.[21]

Nicole Loraux notes some of the more profound implications of these narcissistic male fantasy myths and religious beliefs:

> The doctrine of authochthony is something like the satisfaction of a desire, rather than a misunderstanding of the laws of reproduction. The desire of a society of men to deny the reality of reproduction is vested in the story of Erichthonius, since masculine experience dictates that what really counts takes place among men.... by telling the story of autochthonous origins, the men rid themselves of the opposite sex and exclude all references to femininity from their discourse.[22]

The fifth-century Athenian *polis* was a gender-polarized and segregated society rigidly dominated by masculine values. In such a context, all social conventions, relationships, ideas themselves, acquired gender. The self itself was an exclusively male concept. The gods were not simply male and female but also masculine and feminine, sometimes in contradictory ways. Greek polytheism conveniently allowed for the distribution of gender attributes among different deities. It also created paradoxes, like the androgynous Athena, not only the patron of Athenian women, but also the protector of the city of Athens—the only city in Greece named after a deity—and the personification of skill in warfare. Originally a Minoan deity, Athenian mythmaking masculinized Athena. No one could put it better than she herself does in the *Eumenides*: "I am not of woman born; I am always for the male."[23] In this context, Athena was truly a homogenized goddess, and Aeschylus could confidently call upon her to resolve the gender impasse in the *Oresteia*. That the divine order of Olympus did not reflect the patriarchal values of the democratic *polis* would have been an unthinkable thought in fifth-century Athens.

The world of myth afforded many opportunities to create wish fulfillments, gender fantasies and to exorcize gender nightmares. For example, Zeus, the father and archetype of the patriarchy, had limitless potency, hurled his phallic thunderbolts with impunity and roamed unrestrained in his sexual adventures. Zeus was maleness writ large; rarely did he waste energy on seduction, preferring his sexual conquests in animal form. Masculine superiority had the fiat not only of the state but also of nature and the gods themselves. Zeus, the great potent father, in the realm of myth could also do what no man could do in reality—give birth. Zeus carried the fetus of Dionysus in his thigh and gave birth to the patron saint of tragedy. Even more audaciously, Athena, the patroness of Athens, fittingly and literally, sprouted full-blown from his magnificent male godhead.

With Pericles' new citizenship law of 451 BC, ability to establish paternity became central to the stability of the Athenian political structure. Unlike Zeus, mere mortal men could not give birth, even though at least several male characters in tragedy wished it otherwise:

> JASON. It would have been better far for men
>   To have got their children in some other way, and women
>   Not to have existed. Then life would have been good.
>   (*Medea*, 573–75)[24]

> HIPPOLYTUS. Women! This coin which men find counterfeit!
>   Why, why, Lord Zeus, did you put them in the world,
>   in the light of the sun? If you were so determined
>   To breed the race of man, the source of it
>   Should not have been women.
>   (*Hippolytus*, 615–19)[25]

Outside of Athens and her democratic allies, political power rested only in the hands of the wealthy and important families. Although Athenian political leaders from Themistocles through Pericles came from these same kind of elite families, actual political power in Athens was shared by thousands of citizen families. Because of this, the stability and very existence of the democratic *polis* depended upon its ability to control and determine the status of "citizen." The original democracy of Cleisthenes had been based on the concept of absolute patriarchy and a strict patrilinear family system—any son born to a citizen was eligible for citizenship.

Athens became a multinational melting pot during the fifth century. As it rose in prominence as a shipping and commercial center, the influx of foreigners and immigrants radically escalated. Cleisthenes' sixth-century "antioligarchic" democratic patriarchy was out-of-touch with the new Athens of the fifth century—teeming with thousands of aliens, metics, slaves and foreigners. If the "citizenship question" was not addressed, Athenian citizenship could theoretically expand almost exponentially as immigrants or even slaves married or merely had sex with Athenian citizens. Political and social stability demanded action to restrict and control the status of "citizen."

The Periclean Citizenship Law of 451 BC was designed to restrict permanently the political power base to the pool of existing citizen families. It also inadvertently increased the importance of Athenian women born of citizen families. Citizenship under the new law demanded proof of parentage by both a citizen (father) and a "legitimate wife" (mother) whose father was a citizen. The meaning of this confusing statute is made clear by Simon Goldhill's description of the new definition of citizen as "the male child of a citizen who is married to the daughter of another citizen."[26]

However, the very notion of patriarchy rested upon a fragile and sometimes vexing uncertainty. As any Strindberg male protagonist can tell you, only maternity can be established with absolute certainty. Restrictions upon women's lives and activities were at least partially intended to protect the parental status of the patriarch. Women worked, slept and dined only in the company of other women. Each Athenian *oikos* (household) was divided into sexually segregated quarters. Women never ventured unescorted outside. Since Greek tragedy always takes place in a public setting, usually outside a palace or home—all interior scenes occur "offstage"—entrances of female characters are preceded or followed by an almost obligatory statement explaining why a woman is outside the home or palace.

The new citizenship law severed the logic of the Athenian patriarchy. No longer were all offspring of the father eligible for citizenship. It also drastically increased the value of a select class of women in the society, *viz.* the daughters of citizens. Under the new citizenship law, free-born Athenian women who were daughters of citizens became the most valuable commodity in Athens.

It also introduced many potential elements of uncertainty. Citizenship, open only to males, was a matter of public record that could be checked and verified, whereas, the exact status of a woman could be a matter of question. A woman was enrolled in no *phratrē* (brotherhood) nor registered in the *dēmos*. Furthermore, there were no official written records of marriages.[27] The legality of any marriage in Athens could be challenged at any time, in which case the husband had to produce witnesses who were present at the wedding ceremony. A specific class of women—the daughters of citizens—not only became the most valuable commodity in the city but also *the* controlling factor in the determination of citizenship status and ultimately the source of political power in the *polis*. Surveillance and control of these women became even more important. Ironically, women not born into the privileged citizen families and lower in class and social status enjoyed a level of freedom unknown to citizen-wives and daughters. Likewise, in the nondemocratic city-states, women gained power and influence unheard of in democratic Athens. For eample, even Sparta's institutionalization of both masculine martial values and homosexuality did not lead to contempt or exploitation of women but to their increased freedom from male dominance. In the *Politics*, Aristotle criticized Spartan militarism not on moral grounds but because it allowed women too much freedom:

> Freedom in regard to women is detrimental . . . for they live dissolutely in respect of every sort of dissoluteness, and luxuriously. . . . the inevitable result is that . . . the people are under the sway of their women, as most of the military and warlike races are. . . .[28]

We will never know to what extent the gender antagonism of Greek tragedy reflected any actual or imagined socio-sexual conflicts. One thing is clear, however—sexual conflict and gender antagonism became the major symbolic mode of opposition in Greek tragedy. The "female" as a literary and imaginative concept had barely existed before the fifth-century Athenians. To a great extent, the Athenian tragedians invented the female.

Surprisingly, even though tragedy overdetermined gender in an exclusively male environment, unlike other rituals of male-bonding, the plays did not become venues of mere gender aggrandizement, denigration of the feminine or celebrations of male superiority. Quite the contrary, Greek tragedy characteristically indicted and severely punished gender *hubris*, most especially male gender *hubris*—that is being too masculine. The playwrights always sought the high moral ground in this respect. The acting out and resolution of symbolic gender antagonism and the punishment of gender *hubris* seem to have fulfilled some deep psychic need for Athenian males. It also may have masked or deflected the overt misogyny which many of them may have actually felt.

While Greek tragedy staged the spectacle of the crisis of the democratic patriarchy, fifth-century Athens enacted a world-historical tragedy. The central *agōn* of this tragedy was extreme gender antagonism, and its *hubris* was Athens' increasingly pathologic militaristic androcentrism. The citizens of Athens acted out the crimes and imaginatively experienced the atrocities that are metaphorically represented in the tragedies. The grotesque cruelty of Ajax, the blind androcentrism of Creon, the perverse logic and amorality of Odysseus, the systematic brutalization of the Trojan women, the dismemberment of Pentheus—all of these fantastic mythical aberrations can be reasonably equated to deeds that the Athenians committed in real life. Somehow the male ritual of tragedy seems to have provided Athenian citizens with the *anagnorisis* and cathartic purgation of the gender and social guilt they were denied in real life.

Notes

[1] Richmond Lattimore, trans., *Greek Lyrics*, 2nd ed. (Chicago: University of Chicago Press, 1960), p. 11.

[2] A. T. Murray, ed. and trans., *Demosthenes: Private Orations*, vol. III (Cambridge, Mass.: Harvard University Press, 1939), p. 447.

[3] Mary R. Lefkowitz, trans., *The Lives of the Greek Poets* (Baltimore: Johns Hopkins University Press, 1981), p. 158.

[4] Pickard-Cambridge presents the evidence, pro and con, in *The Dramatic Festivals of Athens*, pp. 264–65.

[5] Roger Just, *Women in Athenian Law and Life* (London: Routledge, 1989), p. 154.

[6] Dorothea Wender, ed. and trans., *Hesiod and Theognis* (Harmondsworth, Middlesex: Penguin, 1973), p. 59.

[7] Nicole Loraux, *The Children of Athena: Athenian Ideas About Citizenship and the Division Between the Sexes*, trans. Caroline Levine (Princeton: Princeton University Press, 1993), pp. 72–110.

[8] Henry George Liddell and Robert Scott, *Greek-English Lexicon*, rpt. 1976 (Oxford: Clarendon Press, 1871), p. 318.

[9] Aristotle, *Nichomachean Ethics*, 1148b.

[10] K .J. Dover, *Greek Homosexuality* (Cambridge, Mass.: Harvard University Press, 1989), p. 16. See also John J. Winkler, *The Constraints of Desire: The Anthropology of Sex and Gender in Ancient Greece* (New York: Routledge, 1990), pp. 45–70.

[11] Aeschines, *Against Timarkhos*, 1.185.

[12] Loraux, *The Children of Athena*, p. 88.

[13] Just, *Women in Athenian Law and Life*, p. 34.

[14] Froma Zeitlin, "Playing the Other," *Nothing to Do with Dionysos?: Athenian Drama in Its Social Context*, eds. John J. Winkler and Froma I. Zeitlin (Princeton: Princeton University Press, 1990), pp. 68–69.

[15] John Moore, trans., *Ajax, The Complete Greek Tragedies: Sophocles II*, eds. David Grene and Richmond Lattimore (Chicago: University of Chicago Press, 1957), p. 32.

[16] Michael Jameson, trans., *Women of Trachis, The Complete Greek Tragedies: Sophocles II*, eds. Grene and Lattimore, p. 111.

[17] Mary R. Lefkowitz, *Heroines and Hysterics* (London: Duckworth, 1981), pp. 14–15.

[18] Xenophon, *Oeconomicus*, 7.22; 7.25. Sarah B. Pomeroy, *Xenophon Oeconomicus: A Social and Historical Commentary with a New English Translation* (Oxford: Clarendon, 1994), p. 143.

[19] Diodorus of Sicily, *Bibliothekē Historikē*, 2.45. Edwin Murphy, *The Antiquities of Asia: A Translation with Notes of Book II of the Library of History of Diodorus Siculus* (New Brunswick, N.J.: Transaction, 1989), p. 58.

[20] Plutarch, *Life of Pericles, The Rise and Fall of Athens*, trans. Ian Scott-Kilvert (Harmondsworth, Middlesex: Penguin, 1960), p. 198.

[21] Simon Goldhill, *Reading Greek Tragedy* (Cambridge: Cambridge University Press, 1986), p. 68.

[22] Loraux, *The Children of Athena*, p. 17.

[23] line 736, my translation.

[24] Rex Warner, trans., *Medea, The Complete Greek Tragedies: Euripides I*, eds. David Grene and Richmond Lattimore (Chicago: University of Chicago Press, 1955), p. 77.

[25] David Grene, trans., *Hippolytus, The Complete Greek Tragedies: Euripides I*, eds. Grene and Lattimore, p. 189.

[26] Goldhill, *Reading Greek Tragedy*, p. 59.

[27] Strangely enough, as Aristotle noted in the *Politics* (1253b), there was no word in classical Greek for "marriage."

[28] *Politics*, 1269b. Aristotle, *Politics*, trans. H. Rackham (Cambridge, Mass.: Harvard University Press, 1977), p. 135.

Chapter Three

Tragedy and Pornography:
Transvestite Ritual Theatre

> MNESILOCHUS. Ah, what soft seductive strains! How feminine, how deliciously voluptuous! What titillation of the senses! Sexy stuff, it does things to you.
> Aristophanes, *Thesmophoriazusai*, 130–33[1]

> The Athenians, then, were the first of the Greeks to make the statues of Hermes with the penis erect.[2]
> Herodotus, *The History*.

Athens, like other Greek cities, had a number of sexually exclusive rituals and festivals. The major Athenian female festival was the Thesmophoria held in October. Herodotus, the friend and contemporary of Aeschylus, claimed that it was established, fittingly, by the daughters of Danaos, mythologized as the original feminist maidens in Aeschylus' *Suppliant Maidens*. Since the festival was open only to women, we do not have a large body of evidence from the male authors of Athens detailing its specific rites or features. It is known that during the three-day Thesmophoria festival women left their homes and camped out at the Thesmophorion, near the Pnyx. Virgins were excluded. One of our most important documents about the festival is Aristophanes' satirical *Thesmophoriazusai* (*Women at the Thesmophoria*), in which the uncle of the playwright Euripides dresses up in drag and sneaks into the Thesmophoria. The male audiences of Athens obviously delighted in the rare glimpse into the secret world of the female rituals of the festival.

Some important features of the Thesmophoria are known. As in the male dramatic festivals, symbols of sexuality and icons of genitalia were very important. H. W. Parke summarizes the information about the central rituals of the Thesmophoria: "The women concerned with the ceremony threw into caverns in the ground various offerings. The chief objects were sacrificial piglets, and also there were models of snakes and male genital organs shaped out of dough."[3] John Winkler explains the meaning:

> Under the obvious concern with promoting fertility there is a structured opposition of the sexes. Women alone conduct the rites; the principal agents must avoid sexual intercourse for three days before their descent. The sacred items are familiar male and female symbols: piglets are a well known stand-in for female genitals and they are thrown into the pits along with phallic cookies.[4]

These female rituals contained at least some vestigial form of "drama," since ritual abuse and indecent language (*aischrologia*)[5]—important ritual features of both the Rural Dionysia and City Dionysia as well as the genre of old comedy—were also central to the Thesmophoria.[6] Indeed, it is possible that the Thesmophoria, "a piece of female counter culture,"[7] as Sue Blundell describes it, included other "dramatic" features. Could the all-female Thesmophoria have been women's answer to the grotesquely male City Dionysia? Since it may have predated the City Dionysia, could theatre owe its origins to the women's festival, from which it incorporated or borrowed essential elements?

The fact that the Thesmophoria was a secret ritual would have seemed appropriately female to Athenian men—women were the silent creatures of Athens. In stark contrast to these private female rites, male rituals and festivals were magnificently public, from the Gymnopaideia in Sparta, where the pubescent boys of the city were paraded naked through the streets before the audience of older men, to the panhellenic Olympic games, where naked men sought to prove their manliness to their fellow males, and, of course, the City Dionysia in Athens.

The City Dionysia publicly celebrated the maleness of Athens. Its participants were all male, and attendance at the plays was primarily if not exclusively male. There is no record of any formal punishment such as the decree of the death penalty for women who attempted to view the Olympic games,[8] but no such sanction was necessary. The presence of a small number of women at the festival would not have undermined its function as a male-bonding ritual but further reinforced it.

Until recently, few critics or scholars have thought it important enough even to allude to the overtly sexual features of the City Dionysia. Those who do write them off as quaint ritual oddities or irrelevant quirks of the Athenian imagination. The fact is that the dramatic festivals were outrageously phallic and masculine, indeed obscenely so by any contemporary standards. A factor that has hindered dissemination of much of this information has been concern for "decency" and "good taste." Even as meticulous a historian and scholar as Arthur Pickard-Cambridge left instructions on his deathbed in 1952, with the manuscript of his unpublished *The Dramatic Festivals of the Athenians*, that "the 'indecencies' should be 'obliterated.'"[9]

The City Dionysia was initiated by a great nighttime public procession (*pompē*) through the streets of Athens. Behind the statue of Dionysus followed the great phallic procession, which included dozens of huge multicolored and elaborately ornamented phalluses carried by the official phallus-bearers (*phallophoroi*) along with ambassadors from all Athenian colonies and allies. As Martin Nilsson describes:

> It [the phallus] was nowhere so conspicuous as in the cult of Dionysus. . . . The colonies of Athens were required to send phalli to the Great Dionysia. The procession at this festival, during which the great works of the tragic and comic poets were performed, would make a grotesque impression upon us if we were able to see it with its many indecent symbols.[10]

Each delegation from the members of the Delian League was assigned its own official phallus based upon the amount of money the "ally" gave to the Athenian military league. Rarely has there been such a precisely literal demonstration of the interconnection of gender, economics and politics. Political prestige and power depended literally upon whose phallus was bigger. The phallic parade was not a symbol of fertility but one of blatant male sexual power and domination. The phallic processions were even more prominent in the less inhibited Rural Dionysia festivals held outside the city each December.

There is no longer any doubt about the importance of the erect phallus to Athenian society and its aesthetic imagination. A number of recently published scholarly and historical works have made available a startling body of visual documentation that has long been ignored or suppressed. Long-held notions of the lofty, Apollonian dignity of Greek art are hard to reconcile with the reality. Eva Keuls claims that the evidence suggests that Athens was—more than a patriarchy or a democracy—a "phallocracy":

> In speaking of "the display of the phallus," I am not referring, as Freudians do, to symbols that may remind us of the male organ, such as bananas, sticks, or Freud's own cigar. In Athens no such coding was necessary. As foreigners were astonished to see, Athenian men habitually displayed their genitals, and their city was studded with statues of gods with phalluses happily erect.[11]

Most prominently, any visitor to Athens would have noticed the thousands of *Hermae* or "herms" that graced every Athenian doorway and each street corner—a statue of the god Hermes with an erect phallus. What was the significance of these phallic totems? Herodotus tells us that Athens was the first city in Greece to install the phallic herms, first displayed in Athens *circa* 530 BC, shortly after the institution of the City Dionysia in 534. Hundreds of years later, Plutarch said that the Greeks of his time found them silly but still continued placing them. Scholars have traditionally interpreted them—when they are mentioned—as crude symbols of fertility. However, as Walter Burkert points out:

> There is not much evidence for the fertilizing power of the herm; herms are not set up in stables or folds, nor in the cornfields, and not necessarily in the bedroom. They stand in front of the house, in the market place, at crossroads, and at the frontiers.[12]

The exhibition of the phallus, according to Burkert, is a primitive and potent masculine display of power, noting that, among primates, "the male delimits his territory by facing outward and displaying his erect phallus."[13]

The erect phallus is not an icon of fertility but an aggressive symbol of male power, an animalistic marking of the boundaries of control. The erect phallus above the doorway of an Athenian home, or on the outskirts of the city, meant: a male rules here, and one who will defend his territory. The masculine nature of tragedy was reinforced, at least in some plays, by the presence of an erect phallus on the altar (*thumelē*) in or near the orchestra.[14]

The herms were the center of one of the most notorious and mysterious controversies in fifth-century Athens. On the eve of the Sicilian expedition, in 415 BC, as Athens prepared to launch its most audacious military adventure of the entire Peloponnesian War, a symbolic political protest occurred. As the expeditionary force marched down to the harbor, the army and citizens were horrified to find that all the herms in the city had been castrated, "mutilated on the same night" as Thucydides recounts. He continues:

> The matter was taken very seriously; for it seemed to be ominous for the expedition and to have been done withal in furtherance of a conspiracy with a view to a revolution and the overthrow of the democracy.[15]

The castrators of the herms were never discovered. Some months later, Alcibiades, leader of the doomed expedition, was accused of organizing the action as well as staging parodies of the Eleusinian Mysteries. The indictment caused him to desert the Athenian cause and take up with the Spartans. However, the accusation was surely a politically motivated ruse orchestrated by Alcibiades' enemies; why would he want to jeopardize the expedition that he had championed in the assembly and of which he was the leader? Eva Keuls suggests that it was the women of Athens who undertook this act of political protest by prominently attacking these symbols of male power that so adorned the city.[16] Whether it was right-wing antidemocrats, peace activists or outraged Athenian women who performed these symbolic castrations, the significance is in the act itself—mutilation of the symbols of masculinity to protest a political and military action. As Thucydides recorded, Athenian citizens instinctively knew the political meaning of the event, and the government feared "revolution" or "overthrow of the democracy." Castrating herms was to strike at the heart of the democratic patriarchy.

The City Dionysia officially opened on the day after the nighttime phallic procession that brought the statue of Dionysus to the outskirts of the theatre. After a night of feasting and drinking, the phalluses were formally paraded behind the statue of the god into the Theatre of Dionysus, followed by a procession, in full dress uniform, of the ephebes, young cadets about to enter military service.[17] The procession also included the twenty dithyrambic choruses of fifty each and the choruses of the plays. The ceremonies proceeded with the blessing and prayer by the Priest of Dionysus, sacrifices at the altar of the god, and addresses by some or all of the ten popularly elected generals. Sometimes, speeches honored Athenian statesmen or war dead. Finally, the male orphans were consecrated—sons of battle-fallen Athenian citizens whom the state had educated, supported and now, on entering manhood, armed as soldiers.

The masculine nature of the festival did not end once the plays themselves started. One special feature of the performances was a central premise of the Dionysian ritual—all celebrants were male, and female characters in the plays were represented by transvestite male performers. The almost universal scholarly and critical silence on this point is astonishing. If tragedy was not conceived of as an exclusively male event, when and how did this "dramatic convention" originate? Did Athenian males consider women incompetent to perform themselves? Was masculine control of the image of the female so important that only males could be entrusted with it? Whatever its origin, Athenian drama is certainly in this regard a direct and exact reflection of the social and political reality. An exclusively male theatre would not seem unusual to a society based on an exclusively male civic world and political system.

What was the logic behind this transvestite ritual theatre? Taking into account the performance demands created by an outdoor theatre that seated over 15,000, it is not likely that any actors could have relied on subtlety or nuance in their performances. The female would always have been exaggerated and overacted; audiences would have seen, not the feminine, but the hyped or hyperfeminine. I do not mean to suggest that the performers in drag would have been considered false or phony by their male audiences. Most of the time, the opposite would probably have been true. Audiences would have been impressed, not with the phoniness of the transvestite performers, *but by how real they seemed*. Just as Elizabethan English audiences felt that their boy actors were better at playing women than the female actresses in the touring Italian *commedia* companies, Athenian audiences no doubt believed their male performers in drag better at playing the female than any woman could be. The "women" in Greek tragedy may have seemed more real to its male audiences than the women in real life.

There is a very precise analogy for this experience and the function of a certain type of tragedy in fifth-century Athens—an all-male audience creating, gazing at and taking aesthetic pleasure in the excessive suffering, punishment and victimization of exaggerated and eroticized representations of the female, or the hyperfeminine. The pattern of a female subjected to extreme violence and put under unrelenting suffering obtains so much in Greek tragedy that it is logical to assume that such representations provided powerful, emotional excitation and maximum "aesthetic effect" for its male audience. As Nancy Rabinowitz asserts, "Tragedy participates in a pornographic structure of representation."[18]

All suffering is not tragic suffering, and all suffering does not arouse the specific aesthetic pleasures and emotional *catharsis* that tragedy did in Athenian men. In order to excite tragic pity and fear, the tragic protagonists—both male and female—were "feminized," that is victimized and made to suffer. In the case of female characters, a special element was often added to heighten these tragic emotions for the male audience—the female was powerfully and provocatively sexualized. Virtually every female protagonist in Greek tragedy is somehow eroticized in order to maximize the emotional effect of the pornography of violence which was a major part of the appeal of tragedy. Note, for example, the mysterious hymn to *Eros* in *Antigone* as Antigone goes off to her death; Deianara hurling herself upon her marriage bed as she thrusts the sword into herself in *Women of Trachis;* the male chorus' erotically charged narration of the slaughter of Iphigeneia as if it were a sexual violation; the perverse description of Clytemnestra's orgasmic sexual release as she slaughters Agamemnon in the *Agamemnon*; Jason's taunts about Medea's (and all women's) uncontrollable sexual appetites. The suffering and victimization of the eroticized female is not incidental but essential to this type of Greek tragedy. Likewise, for a male to be made to suffer as a tragic protagonist—or to express any kind of emotion—he must first be feminized in order to be believable. One of the most important guarantees of reality for audiences was the guarantee of gender reality.

We should not discount the strong possibility that at least some of the female characters in the tragedies were so hyperfeminized that they would have been performed as what we would call "drag queens" (that is "queans" instead of "queens," as Shakespeare would have put it). Certain roles seem to require outrageous characterization. The incessant high tragic lamentations of Medea, Phaedra or Helen, indeed most Euripidean female protagonists, demand to be played in the "grand style"—what some might call camp. Furthermore, male protagonists, such as Eteocles, Orestes, Creon, Hippolytus and Jason repeatedly spew out gender-baiting taunts. Could their gender bigotry not only have been directed solely at the characters on stage but also to the male audience?

> CREON. We must on no account be beaten by a woman. Better to fall
> from power, if fall we must, before a man; and at least we would not
> be called *women's* inferiors.
> (*Antigone*, 678–80)

Even if such declarations are excessive, they still consciously form part of the structure of stereotyped gender logic that underpins the plays, encoding the female as victim and the male as victimizer.

The drag performers apparently developed highly specialized acting skills. The female roles in Greek tragedy have different—and more demanding—requirements than the male roles. For example, almost every lyric monologue—the technically difficult solo arias sung by an actor—is assigned to a female character. This certainly must have been due to the technical expertise of the male actors who played the female parts.

How did this unusual practice of transvestite ritual theatre originate? Phrynichus was the first to introduce "female masks," and I think we can assume that this means that he was the first to introduce female characters.[19] Whatever "tragedy" was under Thespis and Choerilus, it became something very different under Phrynichus after this innovation, one that was even more important than the addition of the second and third actor. The traditional surviving titles of Thespis' plays—*Games of Pelias, Youths, Pentheus*—support the very real possibility that tragedy originally included no female characters.

Perhaps Phrynichus' introduction of the "female mask" to this exclusively male event was even controversial. Could the more overtly masculine satyr plays, with their choruses of males sporting exaggerated phalluses—which was added to the City Dionysia program at about the same time—have been a concession to ruffled traditional male sensibilities when female characters were allowed in the tragedies? Was the later addition of a second dramatic festival (the Lenaea), which centered on comedy where the actors also displayed the exaggerated phalluses, another attempt to reassert traditional "masculine" values in the theatre?

Early tragedy or "lyric tragedy"—tragedy with one actor and a chorus—probably included only male characters. After the creation of the Athenian democratic patriarchy, features from the popular but crude rural Dionsysia were incorporated into the Athenian civic ceremony—the phallic procession and the strengthening of ties to the god Dionysus. As a result, the reconstituted City Dionysia, like the civic and political structure of Athens itself, became much more overtly masculine, a male counterpart to the female Thesmophoria. Finally, Phrynichus' innovation of transvestite performers altered the god Dionysus himself. As previously noted, Dionysus began to be portrayed in artistic representations as an androgynous or bisexual god.

Under the Periclean reforms of the City Dionysia, the phallic procession was made more politically symbolic. It became a public display of Athens' prodigious maleness and a celebration of its domination of the Delian League. What better way for the tribute cities to acknowledge Athenian hegemony than to be forced to publicly parade their smaller, subject phalluses before the citizenry of Athens at their magnificent male civic festival? More than ever, Athens was proud of its great dramatic festivals. After all, as every citizen could see, Athens now wielded the largest phallus in Greece.

Notes

[1] David Barrett, trans., *Aristophanes: The Wasps, The Poet and the Women, The Frogs* (London: Penguin, 1964), p. 105.

[2] Herodotus, *The History*, 2.51.

[3] H. W. Parke, *Festivals of the Athenians* (Ithaca: Cornell University Press, 1977), p. 83.

[4] John J. Winkler, *The Constraints of Desire: The Anthropology of Sex and Gender in Ancient Greece* (New York: Routledge, 1990), p. 198.

[5] Susan Guettel Cole, "Procession and Celebration at the Dionysia," *Theatre and Society in the Classical World*, ed. Ruth Scodel (Ann Arbor: University of Michigan Press, 1993), p. 33.

[6] Bella Zweig, "The Mute Nude Female Characters in Aristophanes' Plays," *Pornography and Representation in Greece and Rome*, ed. Amy Richlin (New York: Oxford University Press, 1992), p. 81.

[7] Sue Blundell, *Women in Ancient Greece* (London: British Museum, 1995), p. 165.

[8] Stephen G. Miller, *Arete: Greek Sports from Ancient Sources* (Berkeley: University of California Press, 1991), p. 99.

[9] T. B. L. Webster, "Note" to Arthur Pickard-Cambridge, *The Dramatic Festivals of Athens*, p. v.

[10] Martin P. Nilsson, *Greek Folk Religion* (Philadelphia: University of Pennsylvania Press, 1961), p. 36.

[11] Eva C. Keuls, *The Reign of the Phallus: Sexual Politics in Ancient Athens* (New York: Harper and Row, 1985), p. 2.

[12] Walter Burkert, *Structure and History in Greek Mythology and Ritual* (Berkeley: University of California Press, 1979), p. 40.

[13] Walter Burkert, *Homo Necans: The Anthropology of Ancient Greek Sacrificial Ritual and Myth*, trans. Peter Bing (Berkeley: University of California Press, 1983), p. 58.

[14] For example Aeschylus, *Suppliant Maidens*, 220.

[15] Thucydides, 6.27.

[16] Keuls, *The Reign of the Phallus*, p. 392.

[17] John J. Winkler, "The Ephebes' Song," *Nothing to Do with Dionysos?: Athenian Drama in Its Social Context*, eds. John J. Winkler and Froma I. Zeitlin (Princeton: Princeton University Press, 1990), pp. 20–62, argues that all the tragic choruses were performed by the ephebes. Although I think this is unlikely, if true, it would have added a further military and masculine aspect to the dramatic presentations.

[18] Nancy Sorkin Rabinowitz, "Tragedy and the Politics of Containment," *Pornography and Representation in Greece and Rome*, ed. Amy Richlin (New York: Oxford University Press, 1992), p. 51.

[19] The Suda, cited in Pickard-Cambridge, *The Dramatic Festivals of Athens*, p. 190.

Chapter Four

"Heifers Trapped by Wolves": Aeschylus' *Suppliant Maidens*

> A woman's fears are always excessive.[1]
> Pelasgos, *Suppliant Maidens*, 503
>
> Obedience to the father is the most important law.[2]
> Herakles, *Women of Trachis*, 1178

The dramatic-poetic universe of Aeschylus is formed of intersecting and contiguous realms. An act of *hubris* in one sphere of the cosmos invites punishment or retribution from another. Xerxes' invasion of mainland Greece across the pontoon bridges constructed over the Hellespont is transformed by Aeschylus in *Persians* from a strategic military maneuver into an impious act of *hubris* that upsets the ecological balance of nature by "yoking" the sea "in shackles like a slave" (745–46):

> From ancient times the gods and fates held sway, and to the Persians was allotted the control of tower-piercing wars and horse-reveling tumults and uprooting of cities;
> But they learned to gaze upon the groves of the sea and the wide-pathed waves whipped white with blustering wind, trusting in thin ropes and man-carrying machines.
> (*Persians*, 100–14)[3]

Likewise, in the *Agamemnon*, the deed that initiates the wrath of Artemis against Agamemnon is not the planned assault on Troy nor the sins of the

House of Atreus but an occurrence in the animal kingdom—the twin omen-eagles' devouring of a pregnant hare—the unholy "feast of eagles" (*Agamemnon*, 137).

The natural world—animal, vegetable and mineral—no less than the supernatural or human, is charged with ethical energy. Appropriately, Aeschylus' plays are filled with striking and sometimes startling imagery. The chorus in the *Seven Against Thebes* thus describes Eteocles' commitment to fight his brother in hand-to-hand combat:

> A stinging desire, like a poisoned fly,
> bites at you even to the mind's dark root,
> goads to a man-lopping harvest, a crimson dye
> of unlawful blood, a vile and bitter fruit.
> (692–94)[4]

There is a mad logic at work in the lyric heights of Aeschylus that often skirts the boundary between the brilliant and the ludicrous. In "thirsty dust, sister and neighbor of the mud" (*Agamemnon*, 494–95), he crosses the line from grandeur to bathos; in Aeschylus, the words can fly up, even when the thought remains below. In his lyric passages, Aeschylus often leaps into pure stream of consciousness, jettisoning syntax and literal meaning. The metaphoric can challenge or overtake reality itself. Birds, fruit, fish, sounds, dust, clothing—the most ordinary—can undergo the most outrageous poetic transformation.

A distinctive feature of Aeschylean dramaturgy was his introduction of a unique form of structure—the connected trilogy, where the action of the single play is subsumed in the larger action of the cycle. The plot in Aeschylus is acted out in the context of a mythic "superplot," similar to what Brian Johnston has termed the "supertext,"[5] a mytho-poetic intertextuality that informs and intersects with the action, such as the House of Atreus in the *Oresteia*, the House of Laius in the *Oedipodeia* (of which the *Seven Against Thebes* survives) or the story of Io in the *Danaid* trilogy (of which the *Suppliant Maidens* is the opening play). Interconnected leitmotifs serve as an imagistic corollary to the superplot, for example, the nautical imagery in the *Seven Against Thebes*, the bird and net imagery in the *Agamemnon*, and the animal imagery in the *Suppliant Maidens*. Details, images and action not only serve their own ends but expand and resonate in the larger context of the superplot. There is no evidence that any other playwright ever composed connected trilogies in this way.

The plays of Aeschylus examine, imaginatively restructure and ultimately legitimize not the ancient myths of a distant past but the great new myth he and other poets and politicians were creating—the myth of the Athenian democratic patriarchal *polis*. The central momentum of Aeschylean dramaturgy is an extreme and ever-widening conflict that threatens the social order and values. Dramatic tension is urgent and immediate because the plays are not really about the mythic past at all. They are formally balanced and controlled debates about the meaning and values of the contemporary Athenian *polis*. Myth is presented in such a way that it challenges a key Athenian institution, and the dramatic action questions a central ideological premise of the *polis*. The resolution of the dramatic conflict is vital to the present and future of its audience of citizens, since things *cannot come to be the way they are* unless the conflict and issues of the play can be resolved. In both the *Oresteia* and the *Danaid* trilogy, there is a synthesis and reconciliation after the universe has been forced to the breaking point. The source of the conflict in both is the premises of gender ideology and the nature of key social-sexual institutions of the Athenian *polis*.

Aeschylus' dramatic world is one of sharp gender opposition. Each of his extant plays have female characters in major and important roles, and five of the seven choruses are female. Even the *Seven Against Thebes*, the proverbially masculine saber-rattling drama,[6] has a chorus of women. The *Danaid* trilogy examines the gender assumptions of the Athenian patriarchy by starkly foregrounding radical "femaleness" with radical "maleness." It challenges the premises of the institution of marriage and the ideology of gender as practiced in the fifth-century Athenian patriarchy by staging a gender confrontation set in the mythic past, one whose successful resolution is necessary in order for the contemporary Athenian *polis* and patriarchy to come into being.

The *Suppliant Maidens* has only recently started to receive the serious attention it deserves. Long thought of as a literary dinosaur, fifty years ago it was hardly considered a play at all. Philip Harsh in 1944 pronounced:

> The *Suppliants* is a play of unusual interest in the history of drama because it represents a transitional period midway between the original lyric dithyramb and classical dramatic tragedy.[7]

Less than a decade later, however, an archeological discovery dated the play between 460 and 465 BC, that is, shortly before Aeschylus' undisputed masterwork the *Oresteia* (458 BC). The new dating of the play sent Greek scholars scrambling. Instead of a juvenile curiosity piece from the late 490s, critics were now confronted with a full-blown "mature" play.

The action of the *Danaid* trilogy reenacts the superplot of the Io myth by the granddaughters of Io. In both, male sexual aggression (Zeus and the Egyptians) and female resistance to sexuality (Io and the Suppliants) are transformed into female acceptance of the now gentle male touch which restores order and balance to the universe. *Suppliant Maidens* stages the return of Io's grandchildren to her native Argos. Danaos and his fifty daughters are fleeing Egypt, pursued by Egyptos and his fifty sons. Danaos, the audience knows, was destined to succeed Pelasgos as King of Argos and establish the line of the Danaians, the ancestors of the Greeks, through his daughter, Hypermestra. The superplot retells the story of Io, who, to satisfy the lust of Zeus, was turned into a cow. Fleeing Zeus' sexual advances and the jealous wrath of his wife Hera, Io wandered the earth tormented by a gadfly. She ended her flight in Egypt, where she finally acquiesced to the will of Zeus.

> Zeus...
> He's bringing you back to your senses,
>   stroking you
> with a hand you no longer fear.
> He merely
>   touches you. Yet that's enough
> to father your black child
> Epaphos (or Touchborn)....
>   (*Prometheus Bound*, 848–51)[8]

Zeus responded—not with aggressive sexual conquest—with tender kindness; he touched her gently, and she conceived the son *Epaphos* ("gentle touch").

In his surviving plays, Aeschylus is almost obsessed with interpreting and reconfiguring the god Zeus. He presented many versions of the godhead—Zeus the omnipotent father, Zeus the tyrant, Zeus the guest-god (*xenios*), Zeus the avenger, and in the *Suppliant Maidens*, Zeus of the gentle touch (*Epaphos*). This trilogy, as much as the *Prometheia*, addresses the evolution of the Olympian Zeus.

The maidens' first appeal to Zeus is in his traditional role of protector of guest-friends and suppliants, Zeus *xenios*. This initiates the dramatic action as they claim their ancestral right as Greek descendants to be protected as "suppliants" at the sacred altar. A new and unique vision of Zeus is presented in the first stasimon (512-97), the Hymn to Zeus *Epaphos*: here, it is not Zeus the avenger of the *Oresteia*, not Zeus the tyrant of the *Prometheus Bound*, nor the Homeric Zeus who hurls the lightning bolt but Zeus of the gentle touch whom the suppliants invoke:

> He sits below the throne
> of no other,
> to no power pays homage,
> does no one's work
> but his own. His deeds are accomplished
> with the whisper of a word
> that brings to birth whatever
> his fertile mind wills.
> (590-97)

Zeus' name is intoned even more than in the *Prometheus Bound*; indeed it is the first word of the play. Aeschylus was concerned with the education of the gods because he was concerned about the education of man. In Aeschylean poetic theology, man creates god. If man was to evolve, then he had to create gods that were more humane and civilized.

Aeschylus apparently ended the *Danaid* trilogy with a grand synthesis that restored harmony to the universe: the transition from the *hubristic bia* (force)—representative of the values of tyranny—to the civilizing influence of *peithō* (persuasion)—symbolic of democratic values of the Athenian *polis*. His Egyptians—both women and men—must be civilized in order for the democratic institution of marriage to be established and the Danaian lineage founded.

Aeschylus, like Shakespeare, never visited Africa. But both playwrights created a mythical Egypt by inverting the "natural" social order and gender ideology of their own societies. In *Antony and Cleopatra*, Shakespeare created a world-historical dialectic between Egypt and Rome; in the *Suppliant Maidens*, Aeschylus created one between Egypt and Greece.

Aeschylean Egypt has turned on its head the reasoned order and stability of the Athenian patriarchy. Egypt is the primitive antithesis of civilized Athens. Egypt—a fictional land-of-upside-down—is marked by dangerous sexual antagonisms and is constructed by a network of inverted gender signs and perversions of social institutions. Whether or not Aeschylus' Egypt was inspired by Herodotus' account in his history, both used the principle of gender inversion to create their versions of Egypt:

> Their [the Egyptians'] habits and their customs are the exact opposite of other folks'. Among them the women run the market and shops, while the men, indoors, weave; ... The men carry burdens on their heads; the women carry theirs on their shoulders. The women piss standing upright, but the men do it squatting.[9]

Sophocles also employed this exact gender inversion:

> Ah! They behave as if they were Egyptians,
> Bred the Egyptian way! Down there, the men
> Sit indoors all day long, weaving;
> The women go out and attend to business.
> (*Oedipus at Colonus*, 337–40)[10]

In *Suppliant Maidens*, this invented Egypt has conveniently perverted all the major patriarchal institutions of the Athenian *polis*—control of women, marriage, fatherhood itself. Instead of the proper female submission and passivity, the gender *hubris* of the daughters of Danaos has made them into feminist maidens, women who hate men, endeavor to "escape the beds of men" (137) and "flee, untamed, unwed" (138), vowing to "choose death, not marriage" (805–06). Maidenly modesty has devolved into fanatical chastity.

Conversely, Egyptian men recognize no restraints in their sexual desires and contacts with women. Animal lust has replaced male courtship; marriage has been replaced by rape:

> Let Zeus see men's insolence [*hubris*] swell, . . .
>   flowering with wanton
> wicked thoughts, frenzied with desire.
>   Lust goads them to ruin:
>   folly traps the fool.
>   (98–104)

The word *hubris*, used often in Aeschylean tragedy, gains special force in this play because it was also the technical Athenian legal term for "rape."

Animal imagery is especially prominent in the *Suppliant Maidens*. The Suppliants are "a flock of doves huddled in fear of hawks" (219–20) and "heifer[s] trapped by wolves" (336); the Egyptians are variously "a raging lustful beast" (759), "mad dogs howl[ing] lecherous at my heels" (890–91), "ravens eager to defile an altar" (750) and "more hateful, more vicious than vipers" (500). The maidens' frenzied imagination conjures up increasingly fantastic bestial metaphors:

>   A huge two-legged snake
>   darts close, eagerly
> lunges at his helpless prey—
>   hideous viper,
>   he grasps my foot in
>   horrible jaws!
>   (914–19)

Family values are especially threatened and perverted. Instead of seeking marriage for his daughters, Danaos orders them:

> Only hold firm to your father's command.
> Honor modesty [that is chastity] more than life itself!
> (1029–30)

Not that the Suppliant Maidens need any encouragement in refusing the advances of the sons of Egyptos—or any men, for that matter:

> May I never,
> Never fall into men's hands,
> under men's power.
> (379-81)

> Better death in a noose's
> embrace than let the man I loathe
> graze my skin with his
> greedy fingers.
> (786-90)

The suppliants rage and wail against "ruthless male pride, swaggering, howling their lust" (817-19). They declare total sexual warfare, vowing a battle to the death with the hated male sex, entreating Zeus to "give women power and victory!" (1088)

In the *Suppliant Maidens*, Aeschylus unleashes a fury of gender antagonism that tears the world apart, creating political, social, sexual and theological crises. Some have suggested that the suppliants "doth protest too much" in their loathing of sex and hatred of men:

> men are
> full of bloodlust, treacherous,
> impure of heart.
> (745-47)

By comparing them to ripe fruit dripping with nectar (1031), Aeschylus seems to drive home this point. However, before we race off to psychoanalyze their childhood anxieties, or diagnose the daughters as suffering from repressed Electral desires or as "archetypal victims of a father fixation,"[11] as Janet Lembke puts it in the introduction to the recent Oxford translation of the play, it is important to reassert that modern notions of character and personal psychology do not apply to the characters of Greek tragedy. There is no psychological "subtext" in Aeschylean drama. Most of the major characters in Greek tragedy can easily be diagnosed as single-minded, excessive or obsessive-compulsive. The reason for this is not neurosis but the nature of tragic character and action. Characters in Greek tragedy are not real people. The tragic protagonists' extremism is the *sine qua non* of tragedy. Simply put, there would be no dramatic action if the major characters were all "normal" or "well adjusted." Furthermore, tragic *hubris* is not simply a crime or an error in judgment; it is the moral arrogance caused by excessive or exclusive commitment to any ideology. As the chorus declares in the *Seven Against Thebes*, "devout men are dangerous" (596). In *Supplliant Maidens*, the maidens' obsessiveness should also reveal that the chorus of Suppliants is the play's protagonist and not Pelasgos, as some have suggested.

These headstrong feminist maidens must have appeared fantastic and outrageous to the original audience. Their strangeness is emphasized by their black skin ("our sun-black tribe," 151) and their bizarre costumes ("robes and headdresses such as no Argive wears, or any woman of Greece," 230–32). They are a far cry from the helpless, defenseless creatures that Athenian men believed their wives and daughters to be. They must have seemed not just from another country but from another planet.

The suppliant maidens have been allowed to cultivate their femaleness *in extremis*. When King Pelasgos approaches, Danaos instructs them: "strike all boldness / from your words, and all immodesty from your eyes" (194–95). Such a command would have been unnecessary for any Athenian women since it means simply "act like women." Three generations removed from the civilized and harmonizing graces of Greek patriarchy, and these maidens are well on their way to becoming full-fledged Amazons. Indeed, this is Pelasgos' initial response to these bizarre African women:

> If you had bows,
> I'd take you for that tribe of husbandless hunters,
> the flesh-eating Amazons.
> (275–77)

If their herald is any indication, Egyptian men are no more civilized than the women, *mutatis mutandis*:

> If you don't give in and move along to the ship,
> I'll have no pity, I'll tear your clothes to shreds! . . .
> I shall have to drag you off by the hair.
> (927–31)

Aeschylus presented human sexuality in terms of a rigid and fixed gender ideology that he manipulated to serve the needs of his dramatic action. He portrayed the nature of male and female sexuality as inherently antagonistic. If society imposed no restraints, the human condition could revert to the nightmare scenarios described in the precautionary myths which told of the times when sexual aggression and gender hostility ran rampant. Women, without the civilizing maintenance and control of the patriarchy, would fall victim to their natural irrationality and their fear of men, as women did in mythical times when rabid packs of feminist Amazons had gutted Attica and subjugated Athens, gleefully raping men and ravaging the land. Men who did not control their aggressive male instincts were also dangerous, and the Greek myths tell numerous stories of unholy bloodlust, rape, butchery and slaughter. Dramatized in this context, as it always was by Aeschylus, the benevolent patriarchy of Athens was both necessary for social stability and beneficial for both men and women. The radical democratic-patriarchal order of Athens is always portrayed by Aeschylus as a compromise and a synthesis, not an extreme.

Pelasgian Argos is a very highly idealized—and very historically inaccurate—version of the archaic predemocratic *polis*. Those who claim that Greek tragedy was not concerned with contemporary politics and issues should note that Aeschylus makes little attempt to produce historical accuracy in the presentation of earlier eras. Euripides was not the first to contemporize the settings and characters of mythology. Pelasgos, even though the very notion of democracy is many centuries distant, is more of a populist democrat than the tyrant or oligarch he would have been. He will make no decision before he can check with his constituency:

> I can promise nothing
> until I share the counsel of all my citizens.
> (352–53)

Most critics regard Danaos as, at best, a simple plot functionary, a static and unnecessary character, evidence of Aeschylus' ineptness in utilizing the second actor, an innovation that, incidentally, he himself had introduced. H. D. F. Kitto, for example, states that "Aeschylus has invented the tool but cannot yet use it properly."[12] It is worth asking why Aeschylus took the extraordinary step of adding the second actor, which changed the entire course of the history of drama, if he did not quite know what to do with him. Danaos' presence is central to the action of the play; in fact, only his presence as the father allows the action to take place and the conflict to be initiated. *Suppliant Maidens* is not a play about fifty women or fifty sisters but fifty daughters. Danaos is a male, and the patriarch of his family. His patriarchal rights as father have been violated. His presence places the action and conflict into a masculine context. Notice that the suppliant maidens do not pray to Artemis or Demeter or Gaia the earth-mother but to Zeus the father. The question in the *Suppliant Maidens* is not women's rights, but male rights, *viz.* the patriarchal rights of Danaos, which have been violated. Danaos brings his own agenda into the conflict, since he has allowed, indeed demanded, that his daughters pursue their strange and unnatural behavior, ordering them to "love chastity more than life."

The second play of the trilogy, *Egyptians*, would force the question of the limits of patriarchal authority even further. We know that Danaos ordered his daughters to kill their husbands on their wedding night, which would have resulted in fifty Clytemnestras with daggers confronting the audience. One of the daughters, Hypermestra, confronts the ultimate patriarchal tragic dilemma—conflicting duties to father and husband. She decided to spare her husband rather than obey her father.

The *Danaid* trilogy, like the *Oresteia*, produces a grand cosmic synthesis. From what we know, the second play presents the death of Pelasgos, the victory of the Egyptians and their seizure of the virgins. Danaos orders his daughters to kill their husbands on their wedding night. All comply, except the future queen of Argos, Hypermestra, who has fallen in love with Lynceus. The final play, the *Daughters of Danaos*, most likely culminates in the trial of Hypermestra, the daughter who disobeyed her father's command. The verdict is rendered by the goddess of love, Aphrodite, and a famous fragment survives that explains her decision:

> Holy heaven longs to pierce the land,
> and longing for marriage seizes earth. Rain,
> falling from the liquid sky, impregnates earth,
> and she, to benefit mankind, gives birth
> to grass for the herds and to grain, Demeter's gift
> of life. From the showers of this wedding flow
> the seasons when trees bear their flowers and fruits.
> Of all these things I also am the cause.
> (fragment 125 Mette)[13]

All the mythic and thematic strands of the trilogy coalesce through the metaphorical power of heterosexual love. Sexuality need not cause conflict and violence—it is the animating and life-giving power of the universe. Men must learn to control their violent instincts, and women must learn to submit to the "gentle touch" of the male in marriage, just as Io was turned from an animal back to a human by the kindly touch of Zeus. By accepting her fate as woman and her gender role as female, Io is redeemed and impregnated. The Suppliants, fleeing the wild beasts goading them, reverse Io's journey, traveling from Egypt back to Greece, and, through the gentle justice of Zeus, will be civilized and integrated into Greek society by accepting marriage and their roles as wives. Thomson suggested that the trilogy ended with the establishment of the all-female Thesmophoria.[14] The institution of marriage is celebrated, according to the principles articulated by Pelasgos, spokesman for Athenian democratic values:

> You shall have
> the women only if they wish so,
> only if honest persuasion wins their consent.
> (961–63)

The *Suppliant Maidens* is not about women's rights or feminism, and it is not addressed to women. It is not concerned with understanding women but defining and controlling the female. Only a supremely confident and self-assured male community could have conceived and produced the *Suppliant Maidens*. The destruction of their patriarchy was not yet a thinkable thought. They were thus able to watch the spectacle of their male institutions and ideology put under the most extreme pressures, questioning and challenges. Finally, they could embrace what had been structured to be, not an extreme position, but the moral high ground of advanced open-mindedness and moderation, which is how they viewed themselves in the safety and comfort of the democratic patriarchy of fifth-century Athens.

Notes

[1] Aeschylus, *The Suppliants*, trans. Peter Burian (Princeton: Princeton University Press, 1991). All citations from this play are from this excellent translation.

[2] C. K. Williams and Gregory W. Dickerson, trans., *Women of Trachis* (New York: Oxford University Press, 1978), p. 67.

[3] My translation. Where no translation is cited, it is my own literal translation.

[4] Aeschylus, *Seven Against Thebes*, trans. Anthony Hecht and Helen Bacon (New York and London: Oxford University Press, 1973). All citations from plays are keyed to the Greek texts.

[5] Brian Johnston, *Text and Supertext in Ibsen's Drama* (University Park: Pennsylvania State University Press, 1989), pp. 67–100.

[6] Aristophanes, *Frogs*, 1020–21.

[7] Philip Harsh, *A Handbook of Classical Drama* (Stanford: Stanford University Press, 1944), p. 44.

[8] Aeschylus, *Prometheus Bound*, trans. James Scully and C. John Herington (New York: Oxford University Press, 1975), p. 71.

[9] Herodotus, 2.35. David Grene, trans., *Herodtus:The History* (Chicago: University of Chicago Press, 1987), p. 145.

[10] Robert Fitzgerald, trans., *Oedipus at Colonus, The Complete Greek Tragedies: Sophocles I* (Chicago: University of Chicago Press, 1954), p. 94.

[11] Aeschylus, *Suppliants*, trans. Janet Lembke (New York: Oxford University Press, 1975) p. 11.

[12] H. D. F. Kitto, *Greek Tragedy* (London and New York: Methuen, 1961), p. 25.

[13] Burian, trans., *The Suppliants*, p. xxi.

[14] Thomson, *Aeschylus and Athens*, p. 308.

Chapter Five

"Not of Woman Born": The *Oresteia*

> We are ruined from within.
> That's what comes from living with women.
> Eteocles, *Seven Against Thebes*, 194–95
>
> This is daring when the female shall strike down the male.[1]
> Cassandra, *Agamemnon*, 1231–32

The *Oresteia* presents a complete example of Aeschylean trilogic dramaturgy. Here, Aeschylus yokes the House of Atreus legend and the Trojan War into the service of the Athenian *polis*. By once again dramatizing and resolving extreme archetypes of gender opposition, he celebrates and legitimizes central institutions of the democratic patriarchy.

The trilogy stages: the murder of the patriarch, the murder of the mother, the trial and acquittal of the matricide. The mythic-political superplot evokes: the crimes of the House of Atreus, the Trojan War and its aftermath, a power struggle between the primitive, chthonic matriarchal deities of an earlier era and the modern masculinized Olympian gods now worshiped in Athens, the final transition in Athens from oligarchy to democracy, and the establishment of the Athenian democratic patriarchy.

The world depicted in the *Agamemnon* is a total inversion of the values of the Athenian democratic patriarchy. A woman rules the city-state, freedom of speech has been suppressed, the city's male elders are subject to the arbitrary rule of a female. This play is an Athenian parallel to films like *Seven Days in May*, *Three Days of the Condor* or Oliver Stone's *JFK*—a paranoid and poeticized rendering of the ultimate political nightmare. As if Clytemnestra's repressive regime is not enough, waiting in the wings is an effeminate tyrant, Aegisthus.

The dramatic axis of the *Agamemnon* is its two antagonists who could not be more dissimilar. Agamemnon only briefly and enigmatically appears, while Clytemnestra is the largest and perhaps the most archly dramatic role in Greek tragedy. Agamemnon is indecisive, Clytemnestra is strong-willed. The *agōn*, which is dramatized through *stichomythia* in the famous carpet scene, captures the essential natures of these two characters:

> CLYTEMNESTRA. He that is not envied is also not admired.
> AGAMEMNON. A woman should not so long for a fight.
> (939–940)[2]

Agamemnon's character has long been the subject of critical debate. Some, like Denys Page, see him as a blameless innocent: "Agamemnon is *compelled, for no fault of his own*, to sacrifice his daughter."[3] Others believe that he is the very exemplar of impious *hubris*, "bearing the full burden of individual responsibility," as Albin Lesky puts it.[4]

It is impossible to find a complete and unambiguous resolution to the question of Agamemnon's guilt or innocence because Aeschylus has characterized him as both guilty and innocent. There is no "right choice" in the dilemma facing him. As presented by Aeschylus, Agamemnon's tragedy is not that he makes the wrong choice, but that he must choose. This he clearly articulates in the chorus' narration of his debate over the fate of his daughter:

> "Heavy indeed my fate if I disobey,
> but heavy, too, if I must butcher my child,
> the glory of my house, polluting a father's hands. . . .
> Which of these two things is without evil?
> How shall I become a deserter of my fleet and fail my allies?
> There is sacred law on their side. . . ."
> (206–14)

This hardly seems the portrait of an arrogant tyrant. And yet, the description of his actions—as opposed to his words—which immediately follows presents a different, if not contradictory, characterization:

> When he put on the harness of Necessity,

> his spirit veered in a breath of change—
> to impiety, to unholiness, to desecration,
> and from it he drew audacity for his heart
> to stop at nothing.
> For indeed there is a wretched distraction of the wits,
> a primal source of ruin,
> that puts recklessness in man's mind
> and counsels ugliness.
> (218–23)

If Aeschylus had wanted to firmly establish the guilt of Agamemnon, he had numerous opportunities. "Which of these two things is without evil?" Agamemnon asks. Readers today may have contempt for Agamemnon's choice of military values over his daughter's life, but we must remember that Aeschylus and his audience would have had little doubt about the importance of military preparedness and martial discipline. Aeschylus' views are here precisely represented by the chorus—like himself, the elders of the city now too old to fight. Aeschylus himself, according to ancient tradition, was more proud of his military accomplishments than his playwriting. His famous epitaph recalled only his bravery on the battlefield of Marathon, not his career as a playwright.[5]

Agamemnon tries to choose the lesser of the evils—if only to avert disaster a little while longer. Granted, only in an extremely masculine-militaristic context could the murder of his daughter be made to seem a lesser evil than disappointing his army. But just as Orestes does in the second play and Athena in the final play, Agamemnon chooses the values of the male over the female. He is punished brutally for his action. However, even with the butchery and sacrilege at Troy, the inherited guilt of the House of Atreus, the murder of his daughter and the defilement of the "female" values of the family, Agamemnon does not emerge as evil. He may be enigmatic but he is not unsympathetic. This alone should inform us that his guilt or innocence is not a central issue of the play. By altering the myth with the addition of Artemis' anger over the "unholy feast of eagles," Aeschylus further clouded the matter of Agamemnon's culpability.[6] The question of "the guilt of Agamemnon" will never be definitively resolved, since Aeschylus portrays him as *both* blameless and guilty. For dramaturgical reasons, Aeschylus intentionally obscured the character of Agamemnon.

In contrast, nothing is obscure, ambiguous or even subtle about Clytemnestra's character or actions. She is a classic example of the dramaturgy of gender inversion. Aeschylus carefully controls our response to her character from the opening speech of the play when the watchman warns us of the "woman's manly-willed (*androboulon*) heart" (11). The reasonable chorus again and again express their displeasure toward, if not downright contempt for, Clytemnestra. Their very greeting of her is worded to express their resentment at the fact that a woman is in charge:

> I have come, Queen Clytemnestra, to pay you my respects;
> for it is right, in the absence of the prince,
> to honor the wife of the man whose throne is empty.
>   (260–62)

When she announces the news of the fall of Troy, the chorus discounts the report because she is a woman:

> CHORUS.   Have you proof of it?
> CLYTEMNESTRA. I have, of course—unless the gods deceived me.
> CHORUS. Dream visions? Do you believe in them?
> CLYTEMNESTRA. No sleeping mind for me, no, nor its fancies.
> CHORUS. Have flying rumors bloated you?
> CLYTEMNESTRA. As if I were a child, you taunt me.
>   (272–77)

The chorus intones a litany of female gender stereotypes—women as gullible, irrational, eager to believe dreams, rumors and gossip:

> It is like the mettle of a woman's spirit
> To praise the gracious gift before it is certainly there.
> The limits of a woman's belief can be
> as easily and quickly crossed
> as cattle graze across a boundary.
> But quickly, too, dies the report
> a woman utters.
>   (483–89)

Contemptuously, she will hurl these words back in their teeth (585–95).

This continuous gender-baiting draws attention to the unusual nature of the current civic-political situation—a woman ruling a patriarchy—while also underscoring Clytemnestra's characterization as unnatural, a woman with the heart of a man. The animal imagery used in the play to describe her vividly reinforces this. Clytemnestra is a veritable menagerie unto herself: a "hateful bitch" (1228), a "double-fanged viper" (1233), a "lioness who sleeps with a wolf [Aegisthus]" (1258–59), a spider weaving a web (1492 and 1516), and a cow who has grown a horn in order to gore the bull (1125). This culminates in Cassandra's torrent of vituperation:

> She is—what shall I call her and be right?
> this monstrous and biting creature.
> A snake with poison at both ends;
> some Scylla living in the rocks, death to sailors;
> some murderous, raging mother of hell;
> some truceless god of war;
> a war she has declared upon her loved ones!
>   (1229–35)

Verbally and structurally, this speech perfectly balances Clytemnestra's ironic welcome of Agamemnon (895–901) and is particularly effective because it is spoken by a female character.

The ostensible action of the *Agamemnon*—the punishment of Agamemnon for his crimes and those of his male ancestors—is undermined by its emotional structure—the unholy murder of the patriarch by the wife. Aeschylus' title character is one of the thinnest and most tenuous pieces of characterization in all Greek tragedy—his eighty-two lines in the longest surviving tragedy are barely enough for a good messenger speech. This ambiguity—I am almost tempted to say absence—of characterization imaginatively deflects any guilt away from him. Agamemnon emerges as essentially a victim of unfortunate circumstances. In contrast, Clytemnestra, structurally the protagonist, is alienated at every turn and never given a moment of sympathy or understanding. Just as Agamemnon's multiple sources of guilt do not tar him as a villain, the multiple justifications for

Clytemnestra's actions do not make her sympathetic. The archetypes being evoked and the signs being manipulated are unmistakable. Whatever its overt dramatic action, Aeschylus exploits male sexual anxieties and turns the emotional structure of the play *against* Clytemnestra. Even though his part is minuscule, the play is appropriately titled *Agamemnon* because the absent father and patriarch dominates the play from its opening speech.

Aeschylus takes every opportunity to undercut potential sympathy for Clytemnestra by identifying female gender transgression as the source of the evils that have been unleashed. The Trojan War—which was proverbially caused by a woman (Helen)—becomes much more prominent than the crimes of the House of Atreus. Aeschylus thus inaugurates what will become a long tradition in the drama of using the Trojan War as a focal point for contemporary political debate.

Clytemnestra's revenge is presented in the most negative terms possible. The unnecessary murder of the innocent and helpless Cassandra is particularly cruel. Cassandra, for all her wild barbarian trappings, is actually a proper Greek woman, and she is presented with enormous sympathy as an archetype of the true female—the passive, suffering victim. Clytemnestra's murder of Agamemnon is committed in a shameful manner, with what the audience would have viewed as characteristic female deception. Additionally, as Apollo points out in the *Eumenides*: "It is not the same for a nobleman to die . . . as to die by a woman's hand" (624–26). Furthermore, Clytemnestra's orgasmic revelry over Agamemnon's body is one of the most blood-curdling moments in Greek tragedy. She sarcastically describes her deed as a grotesque metaphor of the sexual act, one in which Agamemnon ejaculates not sperm but blood:

> So, as he lay there, he gasped out his spirit,
> choking, poured out a sharp stream of his blood
> and struck me with the dark bloody shower.
> I rejoiced as much as the new-sown earth
> rejoices in the glad rain of Zeus,
> when the buds strike in earth's womb.
>   (1390–95)

It is not enough for Clytemnestra merely to kill her husband. This monstrous woman performs a grisly and perverse ritual of purification over his body:

> I threw about him an all-encompassing net,
> as it might be for fish, all-entangling,
> an evil wealth of cloak.
> I struck him twice. He gave two groans,
> and his body went limp;
> as he lay there, I gave him a third,
> in honor of the Zeus that keeps the dead
> securely in the underworld.
> (1382–88)

Clytemnestra is not the only female object of male reproach in the *Agamemnon*. The chorus places the true burden of guilt for the Trojan War and all the calamities that befell the Greeks on another woman, one who does not appear in the play but who is as important as Clytemnestra—her sister and shadow-image—Helen. The war, the carnage and all the impious crimes are blamed on: "a promiscuous [*poluanoros*, lit. a "much-husbanded"] woman" (62, see also 402, 448, 805, 823). There is so much calumny hurled at these two sisters that sometimes it is not clear which one is meant:

> My kindest of guardians has been overcome,
> suffering so much at a woman's hands.
> By a woman his life has perished.
> Curse on you, crazy Helen, that were the single murderess
> of all those lives, those many lives,
> lost under Troy's walls.
> (1450–55)

Characteristically in Aeschylus, an ever-widening chasm opens up between the world of male and female experience, based on the rigid stereotypes of Athenian gender ideology. Agamemnon's choice of a decade earlier is framed in the context of this symbolic gender framework; he must choose between male values (the army, duty to his comrades, concern for the state) and female values (the home, the family, filial affection). He chooses the male. This symbolic gender dilemma and the choice itself—Agamemnon chooses the male, Orestes chooses the male, Athena chooses the male—will be duplicated in each play of the trilogy. The structure of the *Oresteia* is made to appear perfectly symmetrical.

In the first play of the trilogy, a man returns home and is killed by a woman. In the second play, a man returns home and kills a woman. The two women are the same, the two men are father and son. In each the slayer confronts the victim in a climactic exchange. In each the killer gives a speech of justification over the victim's body, claiming the blessing of Zeus and divine justice. The chorus in *Agamemnon* is male; in *Libation Bearers* it is female. The structural similarities in these plays, however, are only superficial. The female chorus in the *Libation Bearers* is sympathetic to Orestes; the male chorus of *Agamemnon* is hostile to Clytemnestra. Even though both use deception to accomplish their revenge, Orestes is portrayed heroically, Clytemnestra shamefully. The action of the *Libation Bearers* fittingly takes place over the grave of the patriarch, and "father" (*patēr*) is perhaps the most repeated word in the play. Orestes' matricide, like his father's slaughter of Iphigeneia, is portrayed as an unfortunate duty forced upon him by the "yoke of necessity." The real question of the trilogy is not who is guilty, but how will Orestes be acquitted?

Not only is Clytemnestra unnatural in her manliness, the mate she has chosen, Aegisthus, is likewise perverse in his womanliness. The chorus addresses him simply as "wife/woman" (*gunai*, 1625) in the *Agamemnon*. Orestes stresses this point in his speech of justification in the *Libation Bearers* when he vows:

> Not to leave the citizens of the most glorious city upon earth,
> the overthrowers of Troy with noble hearts,
> thus to be subject to a pair of women [*gunaikoin*].
> For his heart is a woman's [*thēleia*]; whether mine is, he shall soon
> know.
> (302–5)[7]

This gender-inverted couple is perfectly matched—a woman with the heart of a man and a man with the heart of a woman.

In the *Libation Bearers*, Clytemnestra is portrayed not merely as unnatural; she has now become "the godless woman" [*dustheos guna*;

dustheos gunē] (46, 525). Her revenge has not stopped with the murder of Agamemnon. She has mutilated his body (439), denied him burial rights and imprisoned Electra "like a savage dog" (446). Although Orestes declares that "Might shall clash with might, Justice with Justice" (461), Clytemnestra's claim of justice is a mere technicality. She receives even less sympathy in the *Libation Bearers* than she does in the *Agamemnon*. Not even the female chorus is sympathetic to her point of view—they are loyal to the "true" female, Electra. They declare axiomatically:

> Unions in wedlock
> are perverted by the victory of shameless passion, mastering the female,
> among beasts and men.
> (598–600)

When Clytemnestra finally confronts her son, she remains true to form, calling for her "man-slaying axe" (889). At the climactic moment of the play, in the stichomythic exchange between mother and son, Orestes pauses to remind the audience that, whatever problems a woman might have, they are minor compared to the struggles male breadwinners have to face:

> CLYTEMNESTRA. Name also the follies of your father!
> ORESTES. Do not reproach him who labored, you who sat at home.
> CLYTEMNESTRA. It is a cruel thing for wives to be separated from a husband, my son.
> ORESTES. Yes, but the husband's toil supports them while they sit inside.
> (918–21)[8]

I do not mean to suggest that the *Oresteia* enacts an Athenian male matricidal fantasy or that Aeschylus and his audience were consciously delighting in women-bashing. Quite the contrary, I am sure that both he and his audience would have felt that Clytemnestra's portrayal was particularly fair and objective, given the enormity of her crime—the greatest of all crimes in a patriarchy, the murder of the patriarch. Furthermore, the intensity of the debate would have provided the male citizen audience with an imaginative inoculation against any guilt they might have felt about their gender ideology.

Just as Clytemnestra claimed that her act of regicide would end the cycle of violence, Orestes likewise asserts that the chain of retribution will end with his act of matricide. Aeschylus presents two methods of viewing human history, one cyclical (which he considers archaic) and the other progressive or linear (which he considers modern). In the archaic worldview, echoed by many an Aeschylean chorus, man is trapped within a relentlessly spinning wheel of fortune, a recurring cycle of sin and punishment; justice is a *lex talionis* code of revenge, and wisdom comes only through suffering. However, the Athenian *polis* and its rational male citizen body represent a new vision of history: that man can evolve and choose his destiny, that wisdom can be acquired through knowledge and reason, that a civilized code of written laws can be established. The chorus asks in the closing lines of the *Libation Bearers*, "Where is the end? Where shall the fury of fate be stilled to sleep, be done with?" The answer, of course, is in Athens.

The *Eumenides* concludes in the city of Athens where human destiny has embarked upon a new course. The gender antagonisms of the first two plays erupt into full-scale sexual warfare. The gods themselves join the battle, which pits the primitive female deities the Furies, born of the pre-Olympian earth-mother Gaia, against the modern, rational male gods of the *polis*, sired by Zeus the great patriarch and represented by Apollo. This gender conflict not only threatens the social and political order but religion and theology.[9]

The Furies, as females, argue that the essential familial relationship is blood-kinship and that the determining factor in the family unit is the female—the mother who carries the child inside her. Thus, the ties of mother and child, who have shared the same body, and of brother and sister, who have shared the mother's body, are not merely sacred but the only legitimate blood-family relationships. This is the logic of matrilinear descent, the system, which had been practiced at Crete during the Minoan civilization a millennium earlier, where female deities were supreme, the mother was considered the primary parent, and lineage and property passed through the mother, not the father.

That their ancestors had worshiped female deities in a matrilinear system would have been an unthinkable thought to fifth-century Athenians, but they, nevertheless, must have realized that only maternity could be determined with absolute certainty. Indeed, the maintenance of the patriarchy necessitated ever-increasing measures to physically control, restrict and "protect" women in order to ensure the illusion of the "certainty" of paternity.

The Furies assert a strict matrilinear interpretation of the family as a blood-kinship, insisting that the father is not a blood-kinsman and thus not a true parent:

> CHORUS. We drive from their homes the killers of their mothers.
> APOLLO. And what of a woman who has slain her husband?
> CHORUS. That would not be the shedding of one's own blood with
> one's own hand.
> (210–12)[10]

Biology might prove that the mother is the only certain parent, but Athens was a patriarchy based upon patrilinear descent. The older matriarchal concept of blood-kinship was not only antithetical to the patriarchy but also to the democracy, which had struggled to transform the family into a political unit. No doubt the audience knew, or at least expected, that the values of the democratic patriarchy would ultimately be upheld in the trilogy, but how could the values of the patriarchy be reconciled not only with reason but with the lofty Aeschylean ideal of justice?

Apollo, in defending the patriarchy, maintains that the civic bond of marriage takes precedence over the familial bond of blood-kinship, that "the marriage bed, granted by fate to man and woman is mightier" (217–18). The Furies respond by invoking religion and theology to support their claims for matrilinear kinship, citing mythological precedent:

> It is the father's fate of which Zeus reckons most, by your account;
> yet he himself bound his aged father, Kronos.
> Does not this argument of yours fit ill with that?
> (640–42)

In response, Apollo makes his famous declaration of male supremacy:

> She who is called the child's mother is not its parent, but only the nurse of the newly implanted seed. The parent is the male. . . . And I shall offer proof of what I say. There can be a father without a mother.
> (658–63)[11]

Apollo counters the Furies' final argument by citing Zeus' birthing of both Athena and Dionysus. This does not win the debate—it causes a stalemate. Religion and mythology cannot resolve the gender conflict, because mythology is contradictory. The court is deadlocked.

A manly woman (Clytemnestra) had initiated the action of the trilogy; another manly woman (Athena) will now end it. Athena, a unique deity (because she had no mother), casts the tie-breaking vote with the famous declaration: "I am not of woman born; I am always for the male" (736–37). Athena is the only goddess who can make such a statement, which would have been particularly appropriate in the Theatre of Dionysus, since a male actor spoke from behind the female mask. Athena concedes that the claims are equal, but she admits her bias and casts her vote accordingly.

But Athena's resolution of the tragic conflict is not simply the assertion of masculine prerogative. The wisdom of Athena, daughter of Olympian Zeus, is that justice demands not fanaticism but compromise. She declares that the female spirit, represented by the Furies, must not be ignored or dishonored. Athens, like its namesake goddess, is "always for the male," but she cautions the citizens that male arrogance or gender *hubris* will lead to destruction and chaos. From now on, reason and rational discourse, not blood vengeance, will rule in the city of Athens. The female deities will have their own services, sacred space and place of honor if they abandon the tactics of gender confrontation and learn the masculine and democratic art of "persuasion" [*peithous*] (885–87).

A central aspect of the *Oresteia* as a political instrument was the fact that Aeschylus placed it in the context of one of the most radical and controversial reforms of the Athenian democrats—the dismantling of the power of the aristocratic Court of the Areopagus. Under the oligarches and the tyrants, the Areopagus had ruled supreme in all cases. But four years before the *Oresteia*, in 462 BC, the Areopagus had been relegated to little more than symbolic status with the limitation of its jurisdiction to the crime of murder alone. The powers stripped from the Areopagus had been transferred to the democratic institutions of the *boulē* (council), the *ekklēsia* (assembly) and the popular law courts. As evidence of the bitterness of the controversy, Ephialtes, the radical democrat who had championed these changes, was not present to see his reforms poeticized by Aeschylus. He was assassinated in 461 BC, and succeeded by the young Pericles.

As a fitting piece of irony, the Areopagus met and held its sessions on the hill where the Amazons, the original gender transgressors, had supposedly camped out and perversely worshiped the god of warfare and maleness, Ares. The *Oresteia* mythologizes and celebrates the ascendency of the patriarchy and the Athenian democracy, which was transforming not only the world and its ancient institutions but also the gods themselves into its image and likeness. The *Oresteia* says farewell to the Areopagus—the last great institution of the predemocratic era. Athena synthesizes and clarifies all the social, moral and political themes of the play, while giving the citizen audience a veritable civics lesson:

> Hear now my ordinance, people of Attica,
> you who are trying your first trial for the shedding of blood.
> In future times also there shall remain for the people of Aegeus forever this
>   council of judges
> And this hill of Ares, where the Amazons had their seat
> and pitched their tents. . . . In this place shall the awe
> of the citizens and their inborn dread restrain
> injustice, both by day and night alike,
> so long as the citizens themselves do not pervert the laws
> by means of evil influxes; for by polluting clear water
> with mud you will never find good drinking.
> Neither anarchy nor tyranny shall the citizens defend and respect,
>   if they follow my counsel.
>   (681–96)

In the *Oresteia*, Aeschylus set himself the challenge of rewriting mythology in order to legitimize the social-sexual text of the Athenian *polis*. He marshals all his grand poetic powers to resolve the gender confrontation and to poetically empower the democratic patriarchy. The brilliant but fragile Aeschylean poetic-political synthesis restores harmony to the cosmos and holds the fractured universe together—it bends but does not break.

Notes

[1] Richmond Lattimore, trans., *Agamemnon, Aeschylus I*, ed. David Grene and Richmond Lattimore (Chicago: University of Chicago Press, 1953), p. 74.

[2] David Grene and Wendy O'Flaherty, trans., *The Oresteia* (Chicago: University of Chicago Press, 1989), p. 65. All translations from the *Agamemnon* are from this edition.

[3] John Denniston and Denys Page, eds., *Agamemnon* (Oxford: Clarendon Press, 1957), p. xxiii.

[4] Albin Lesky, *Greek Tragedy*, trans. H. A. Frankfort (London: Ernest Benn, 1965), p. 74. For a full discussion of this question, see D .J. Conacher, *Aeschylus' Oresteia: A Literary Commentary* (Toronto: University of Toronto Press, 1987), pp. 85–92.

[5] *Life of Aeschylus* 2.24–25: "This tomb in grainbearing Gela covers an Athenian, Aeschylus son of Euphorion, who died here. The famous grove of Marathon could tell of his courage and the longhaired Mede knew it well." Mary R. Lefkowitz, *The Lives of the Greek Poets* (Baltimore: Johns Hopkins University Press, 1981), p. 159.

[6] In the traditional version of the myth, Artemis is angered because Agamemnon boasts that he is a better archer than she is.

[7] Hugh Lloyd-Jones, trans., *Aeschylus: The Oresteia* (Berkeley: University of California Press, 1993), p. 147. All translations cited from the *Libation Bearers* are from this edition.

[8] This exchange is possibly parodied in Euripides' *Electra*, 73–79.

[9] These issues are examined in Michael Gagarin, *Aeschylean Drama* (Berkeley: University of California Press, 1976), pp. 87–118.

[10] Hugh Lloyd-Jones, trans., *Aeschylus: The Oresteia* (Berkeley: University of California Press, 1993), p. 222. All translations from the *Eumenides* are from this edition.

[11] My literal translation.

Chapter Six

A Woman's Place Is in the Tomb: Sophocles' *Antigone*

> Outside things are a man's concern.
> Let no woman debate them.[1]
> Eteocles, *Seven Against Thebes*, 200–01

Conflicts between the family and the state recur often in Greek tragedy. The creation of the democratic *polis* had been at the expense of tribal power and familial loyalties. The centerpiece of Cleisthenes' democratic reforms (508–503 BC) was the reorganization of the Athenian tribes. He expanded them from four to ten but, more important, changed the tribes from familial units related by kinship to mere political entities. The ten new tribes were organized according to geographical *dēmoi*, similar to modern American political "wards" or districts, instead of the traditional blood-familial units based upon the *genē* (family) and *phratrē* (brotherhood).

Both oligarchy and aristocracy depended on extensive family and kinship ties, and political power rested in the hands of a few closely knit families. The democracy broke up this political monopoly, lessened the importance of the traditional family structure and widened the political power base. The basic political unit of the democracy became the individual citizen and his *oikos* (household), not the large extended family. The state assumed many duties that had previously been the domain of the family. For example, in the predemocratic era the deaths of important Athenians were mourned at lavish family-sponsored funerals funded by prominent family members or blood relatives. By the time of Pericles, the funerals of important citizens had become public civic spectacles, organized and financed by the state.

Hegel was the first to identify an ideological conflict as the center of the play's action: "The public law of the State and the instinctive family-love and duty towards a brother are here set in conflict." He went on to locate the nature of this struggle in the sociological assumptions of gender: "Antigone, the woman, is pathetically possessed by the interest of family; Creon, the man, by the welfare of the community."[2] Creon could hardly have described the rigid gender polarities of fifth-century Athens any better. *Antigone* sets in motion a dialectical opposition between two central Athenian institutions—the family and the state or *polis*.

Hegel's influential analysis helped place *Antigone* at the center of the modern discourse on Greek tragedy, and throughout the twentieth century, it has been regarded as one of the most "timely" and "accessible" of all Greek plays. It is also considered the most overtly political. Interestingly, the symbolic importance of burial rights for "enemies of the state" continues to animate political causes from Palestine to Ireland. Antigone has been romanticized into an icon of revolt, her very name synonymous with heroic resistance to oppression and her burial of Polyneices applauded as the paradigm of all civil disobedience. The title character defies the tyranny of the state and lays down her life for her principles. However, before we wax too eloquent on the play's revolutionary cachet, it is important to examine the significance of the play not in terms of twentieth-century politics but in the context of mid-fifth-century Athens.

Although the play's action initiates a potentially subversive political conflict, Sophocles does not empower or even articulate any specific ideology as the source of Antigone's actions. In fact, her explanations and justifications remain notably vague throughout the play. Sophocles withholds audience sympathy from Antigone by isolating and distancing her character while gradually but relentlessly foregrounding Creon's character and privileging his tragic discourse and perspective. Certain features, long described as "structural flaws," are evidence of Sophocles' attempts to control or repress the political subtext and neutralize the ideological discourse of the play. Antigone is not, nor was she intended to be, a self-conscious feminist or heroic revolutionary. She is actually a rather conventional sign of the female, created by inversion, negation and antitype. Her character conforms to expected male stereotypes of gender; it does not challenge or question them.

Most of the females in Greek tragedy do not exhibit the qualities that women were expected to possess in real life. Just as the male characters who enter the tragic arena are usually transgressors or criminals, female characters usually violate the norm. Often they are gender transgressors, as Aeschylus' Suppliant Maidens and Clytemnestra—unnatural perversions of the gender female. Such gender encoding operates dialectically—to identify improper female behavior or to define the inverted or negative sign of the female is likewise to identify proper female behavior and to define the positive sign of the female. To reinforce or highlight this gender coding, a correct sign of the female—a meek, suffering victim—is often placed next to the inverted sign. This is the reason for Chrysothemis' presence in the *Electra* and Ismene's in the *Antigone*, to give two examples from Sophocles.

As a trope of victimization, the female held enormous possibilities for eliciting pathos and emotion from its masculinized citizen audiences. Throughout its history, western drama has exploited for sympathy on the stage characters who in real life are systematically marginalized and oppressed, and Greek tragedy was no exception. Because women in real life were politically powerless and could easily be subjected to extreme victimization, the female was an especially useful metaphor for the fragility of human experience. When it served his dramaturgical purposes, Sophocles knew how to exploit the sign of the female in this way as well as any Greek tragedian, as this example from his lost play *Tereus* shows:

> PROCNE. I am nothing. . . . The female sex is nothing. When we are children . . . our life is the most pleasant in the world; young girls grow up in thoughtless delight. But when we reach maturity and intelligence, we are expelled, bought and sold, far away from the gods of our parent, some to barbarians, some to houses where everything is alien, others to houses where they meet with hostility. But all this, when one night has joined us to our husband, we must acquiesce in, and pretend that all is well.[3]

Just as the masculine engine of the state machinery crushes her, the dramaturgy of the play is turned against Antigone. Contrary to standard assumptions, Sophocles did not attempt to privilege Antigone's point of view—if indeed one can even identify such a thing as her point of view—and he certainly did not intend to challenge or question the dominant male democratic ideology of the *polis*. On the contrary, he employed every dramatic strategy at his disposal to neutralize the play's initial conflict, control the ideological discourse and deflect the action away from its potential subversive implications. In order to accomplish this, he was forced to shift the focus of dramatic action away from Antigone and toward Creon.

Despite Hegel's pronouncement of the play as the "supreme and absolute example of tragedy,"[4] many have found structural failings in the *Antigone* and other "early" plays, such as the *Ajax* and the *Women of Trachis*. The term "diptych" has been used to describe these plays in which the action seems to be divided into two parts.[5] Examination of the *Antigone* as a diptych leads to many interesting observations. The title character only appears in the prologue, two of the five episodes and one choral song. She exits long before the end of the play (line 943), never to appear again. Her role is dwarfed in number of lines by Creon, and she does not have a chorus sympathetic to her point of view, which we would expect if she were the protagonist. Throughout the play, Antigone remains isolated.

Viewed as a diptych, *Antigone* is a sophisticated and advanced example. In the *Ajax* and the *Women of Trachis*, there are very obvious breaks where the action shifts. But as A. J. A. Waldock notes: "What we have in the *Antigone* is an imperceptible glide—a hidden shift from one theme to another."[6] By dramaturgical sleight of hand, once Antigone has served her dramatic function of triggering Creon's intransigent *hubris*, she is pushed aside, subtly perhaps but unmistakably. This is not a structural flaw but evidence of the most advanced dramatic artistry.

The *Antigone* is an impressive example of a structure based upon an important Greek philosophical concept—unity through conflict. It is the great play of antitheses. Two unbending monoliths are placed on a collision course. Each propels the other forward in a complex tragic symbiosis. The dual protagonists are swept up in a swirling maelstrom of antitheses: male/female, state/family, old/young, public/private. Creon invokes the gods above (the Olympian gods), Antigone the gods below (the chthonic deities); Creon seeks to control and subjugate nature, Antigone yearns for fusion with nature; Creon's language is appropriately filled with images of power and control, especially the vocabulary of technology, metallurgy, and animal subjugation.[7]

The *Antigone* is held together by its oppositions, and the axis of these complex antitheses is gender. Its two main characters are created by exaggeration and manipulation of gender ideology. In Athens the woman's sphere was exclusively domestic—the home and the family. Antigone defends this traditional female terrain with ferocity. Creon is equally committed to preserving masculine exclusivity in the civic and political spheres, extending this control to include the family unit. Antigone stumbles into the male realm of politics; Creon ventures into the female terrain of the home and family. Antigone's fate is the pathetic tragedy of a victim. Creon's is the sentimentalized tragedy of the patriarch. Antigone fails in the world of politics because, in Athenian politics, women did not exist, either realistically or imaginatively. As already noted, the word for citizen simply has no feminine form. Conversely, Creon's failure is domestic, not political. He fails not in running the state but as the patriarch of a family.

For Creon, an overdetermined sign of the male, the play's action quickly narrows into a power struggle based on the ideology of gender. Creon proclaims what was every Athenian male citizen's birthright: "While I am alive no woman [*gunē*] shall rule me"[8] (526). The boundaries between gender and politics rapidly blur in Creon's increasingly extremist rhetoric:

> Thus the appointed rules must be upheld, and we must on no account be beaten by a woman. Better to fall from power, if fall we must, before a man; and at least we would not be called *women's* inferiors.
> (677-80)

The androcentric arrogance of Creon's extremist gender *hubris* is his *hamartia*. When the patriarchal authority of "father" does not persuade his son Haemon, Creon appeals to him by trying to relate "man-to-man": "Never, then, my son, for the sake of pleasure, discard your good sense on account of a woman" (647–50). When this approach also fails, Creon resorts to shameless macho taunts—"You vile creature, giving way to a woman" (746)—and calls his son a "woman's slave" (756). Haemon, however, is neither cajoled nor bullied into sharing Creon's misogyny.

Creon's contempt for the female is graphically underscored by his crude response to Ismene's question about Haemon's betrothal, which Andrew Brown calls "perhaps the coarsest line in Greek tragedy"[9]: "Others have furrows that can be plowed" (569). Playing on a relatively common metaphor for marriage, Creon turns it into a crude "locker-room" joke, startling in the dignified context of tragedy. Perhaps this even elicited a laugh from some of the male audience. Creon's continuous gender-baiting certainly presented many performance possibilities for the actor.

Creon, fittingly representative of the political reality of fifth-century Athens, becomes more and more obsessed with the ideology of gender. All issues—political, moral and ethical—become reduced to one issue alone: "Now I swear that she is a man and I am not, if she is to prevail in this and go unpunished" (484–85). Creon starkly illustrates the reality of the politics of gender when he orders the arrest of Antigone and Ismene with the words: "From now on they must be women [*gunaikas*]" (578–79).

Antigone and Creon represent two opposing gender-determined readings of the institution of the family, just as the Furies and Apollo had. In the *Oresteia*, the man/woman Athena had stepped forward to resolve the tragic impasse and legal deadlock. However, no compromise or synthesis is possible in the world of the *Antigone*. The action of the play reenacts the tragic paradigm of the House of Oedipus—the family destroys itself. Antigone dies husbandless, fatherless, brotherless. Her mother's brother Creon causes the death of his legal heir and legal wife.

For Sophocles' male citizen audience, Creon's values were not wrong; they were just too extreme. Indeed, his opening declaration of the ideals of the democratic *polis* was later quoted in a speech by Demosthenes to illustrate civic virtue. Creon was masculine superiority writ large, a poetic overstatement of the values of the patriarchal Athenian technocracy. Ironically, Athens itself is inflicted with the same *hamartia* as Creon—an increasingly paranoid androcentric gender *hubris*—and historically will follow Creon's course of action with similar results.

Creon's extremist gender ideology leads not to order but chaos, and his initial exuberant self-confidence degenerates into shameless *hubris*. Speech by speech he grows tyrannical. He begins as the calm, rational technocrat; by the end he is raving as hysterically as the female chorus of *Seven Against Thebes*. This reversal of expected gender behavior would not have been lost on the original audience nor would the irony of his frantic rush to perform the "pure rites of washing" (1201) on Polyneices' body, which was traditionally performed by the female family members. The great macho tyrant finds himself, finally, reduced to woman's work.

Antigone, from the perspective of the fifth-century male Athenian, suffers the ultimate tragedy for a woman by dying unmarried and childless. She enters a tomb instead of a bridal chamber, "a bridal room of death" (1206), and she sleeps with death instead of a husband. This is not merely an aesthetically clever displacement by Sophocles but a means of making Antigone psychologically believable in terms of contemporary Greek medical theory. Hippocrates, the great physician of the classical age and the father of medicine, identified a new disease that young unmarried women were especially susceptible to: hysteria. Besides anorexia, its symptoms included the following: (1) "the girl goes crazy"; (2) "the girl says dreadful things"; and (3) "a desire [*eran*, verbal form of *eros*] sets in which compels her to love death." Like Antigone, these young unmarried women were a danger both to themselves and to others. The only cure was to "cohabit with a man as soon as possible. If they become pregnant, they will be cured."[10]

The Chorus soberly tells us, "No one is so foolish as to desire death [*thanein erai*]" (220). Yet, Antigone dares Creon to carry out the edict and execute her—"Why do you delay?" (498–500) she taunts. Antigone is committed to her desire to die, as she puts it: "Acheron will be my bridegroom" (816). The linking of sex and death is underscored in the third stasimon (781–800), the "Hymn to *Eros*," immediately before Antigone's final appearance. The meaning of this ode and its relation to the action of the play, long a subject of controversy, refers very specifically to Antigone's "hysteria" and her unnatural and perverse passion to die. Furthermore, the imaginative linking of sex and death eroticizes the virginal and previously desexualized Antigone for the male audience. It adds a sexual quality to the normal tragic emotions and aesthetic delight.

The significance of Antigone dying husbandless, as she puts it, "deprived of bridal bed and wedding song, having no portion of marriage or the raising of children" (918–21), should not be underestimated. As Jean-Pierre Vernant explains, "Marriage is for the girl what warfare is for the boy. For the young girl emerging from childhood it represents the normal goal of her sex, access to full femininity."[11] In terms of the male imagination and gender ideology of fifth-century Athens, Antigone's life is meaningless, a total waste. She dies a zero, a nothing.

Antigone is a construct of negation. She is, above all, the great no-sayer. As R. P. Winnington-Ingram puts it, "She rides into the play on a torrent of negatives,"[12] using eight negatives in the first six lines of the play. As female, that is as the "other than male," Antigone is defined not by what she stands for but what she stands against. Fittingly, Antigone champions "the gods' unwritten and unfailing rules" (456–57)—an obvious contrast to one of democratic Athens' greatest achievements, written laws visible to all. As a female, Antigone's essence is her inarticulateness—she cannot articulate an ideology any more than she can define an identity. The closest she comes to an explanation of her moral or philosophic principles is the declaration, "It is not my nature to join in hatred, but in love" (524). This cryptic aphorism, however, is profundity itself compared to her "deathbed speech," which Michelle Gellrich appropriately characterizes as "an awkward, ill-fitting piece of sophistry."[13] Antigone's final statement of justification (905–12) is so convoluted and obtuse that most scholars challenge its authenticity and excise it from the play. The great Sophoclean editor and scholar Sir Richard Jebb believed that her sentiments were "unworthy of Sophocles."[14]

> My husband being dead, I could have another, and a child by another
> man if I had lost a child; but as my mother and father are hidden in
> the house of Hades, no brother could ever be born again.
> (909–12)

The problem is that Antigone has no philosophy or ideology to articulate. As the etymology of her name suggests, she is the "antagonist"; she does not stand *for* anything, she stands *against* things. Here, as often in Greek tragedy, the sign of the female is primarily defined not by what it is but by what it is not.

Antigone is not meant to be an exemplar or spokesperson for Greek womankind. Lest we get the wrong idea, Sophocles places next to her another sign of the female—a gender *raissoneur*, a proper example of the gender female—her sister, Ismene. Ismene knows her place and knows "first that we are women, not meant to fight against men" (52). Her presence helps further distance Antigone from the audience: even though she is supposedly the great champion of family values, Antigone treats her sister almost as badly as Creon treats his son (526–81).

The male chorus of the play is another integral part of Sophocles' strategy for alienating Antigone. The chorus is certainly not there to commiserate with or for Antigone nor to present her case to the audience. Indeed, the chorus stubbornly sides with Creon until almost the bitter end. Even as Antigone goes to face her death, they lecture her: "Breach of authority cannot be tolerated by one in whom authority resides. Your self-willed temper has destroyed you" (874–76). These sentiments could hardly be topped by Creon himself.

The major dramaturgical shift in the play's action occurs after Antigone's final exit, following the agitated lyrics of her *threnos* (lyric ritual lament). Audience attention is at this point focused on an overwhelming dramatic question: What will happen to Antigone? Will she be saved (as she was in Euripides' later version of the myth), or will she die? By the entrance of Tiresias, Sophocles has shifted the central dramatic question to: Will Creon change his mind? At this point, Sophocles unleashes a breathtaking flurry of events and a rapid sequence of dramatic reversals. Out of nowhere appears Eurydice, "coming from the house," as the chorus tells us, "either by chance or on hearing the name of her son" (1181–82). A scant ninety-four lines later she is dead, the shortest life of any speaking character in Greek tragedy. Sophocles has invented Eurydice (she, like Haemon, is not part of the myth) solely in order to kill her off. By creating a nuclear family for Creon, Sophocles further undercuts Antigone as potential protagonist. The deaths of Antigone, Haemon and Eurydice follow one upon another. Haemon's body is brought before the audience. Eurydice's body is dragged out. The action has changed focus so completely that no one thinks to ask what has happened to Antigone's body? Antigone does not simply die—she is erased. Fittingly, the play ends with the chorus lamenting Creon's horrible and terrifying fate.

The dramaturgy of *Antigone* is designed to displace the title character as protagonist, centering more and more on Creon—his mistakes, his failings, his *hubris*, and it is ultimately his tragedy. Creon usurps the tragic action of the play, and his fall, which occurs before our eyes, dominates. All the major reversals of action occur in relation to him, not Antigone. Antigone gains no tragic insight, she makes no mistake or error in judgment. She is the catalyst that initiates the chain of events that ends with the destruction of Creon and his family line. No less than Eurydice, Antigone too is there finally to die. Woman's place is in the tomb.

Despite the potentially dangerous ideological confrontation implicit in the opening, by the end we are left with the hardly profound insight that moderation is the best course and that it is important to find a proper balance between leadership and tyranny. The chorus is so conservative that it even starts to sound like Aeschylus. Andrew Brown says of the second stasimon that "it is almost more Aeschylean than Aeschylus":[15]

> Happy are they whose life has no taste of evils. For, when the gods make a house to tremble, all manner of disaster attends its members, visiting the whole company of the race; just as the swell of the open sea, when it runs before a cruel Thracian wind across the Stygian

depths, churns the black sand from the bottom, and the cliffs to
leeward roar with pain at the storm.
(582–93)

Although his original motives had seemed noble enough, Creon quickly degenerates into a headstrong and unbending tyrant. Tyranny was despicable to the Athenians, and Creon is a tyrant, as both Antigone (506) and Tiresias (1056) explicitly point out. Creon's tyranny, however, does not destroy the state—it destroys his family by robbing him of a male citizen's two most valuable possessions, his legal wife and his heir. The family is Creon's problem, and the play centers on the meaning of the family unit within the new political structure of the patriarchal democratic *polis*.

The dominant ideology of the democratic patriarchy is not undermined in the *Antigone*; no fundamental values are questioned; no progressive notion of either woman's rights or individual freedom is put forward. The most advanced aspect of the *Antigone* is its technique. The enormous ideological questions latent in the play's conflict remain merely implicit. Sophocles spends his aesthetic energies deflecting and controlling them not exploring them. The famous Sophoclean irony is as much an ideological tactic as an aesthetic device. However, the very fact that Sophocles can manipulate moral attitudes so deftly, that terms like *dikē* (justice) and *nomina* (laws) can be used so ambiguously, or at different moments with opposite meanings, expose the moral and ideological anxieties that he worked so hard at sublimating. Conversely, the fact that the dominant ideology does not have to be articulated—as it must be in Aeschylus, for example—is evidence of the audience's absolute faith and belief in those values. Sophoclean tragedy ultimately gains its great power from the sense of the inevitabilily of the values and ideology of the democratic patriarchy. In Aeschylus, man can break free and choose his destiny. In Sophocles, man must bend to the inevitable—"the way things are" have become "the way things have to be."

Sophocles' ability to manipulate ideological discourse at least partly explains why he won eighteen first prizes at the City Dionysia—far more than any other playwright—and Euripides only four. Sophocles, a friend of

Pericles, was a completely invested and privileged member of the patriarchy. The type of social "questioning" found in *Antigone* was both safe and flattering. Antigone's fate was not a rallying cry against injustice but actually imaginatively empowered the authority of the democratic patriarchy's hegemonic discourse. Creon's fall had not questioned the political system but cautioned on the abuse of power. No values of the dominant ideology are ever imaginatively threatened. Not even its blatant androcentrism is questioned; instead we note that Creon takes his misogyny too far.

Creon is not tricked or duped. His family is destroyed because he makes very bad choices and acts very unwisely. The male citizens of Athens could all applaud themselves, self-assured and self-satisfied in their androcentrism, convinced that they were "enlightened" and "progressive." Indeed, had they not wept for and taken aesthetic delight in the sufferings of the poor Antigone? Had they not finally disapproved of Creon's fanatical androcentric extremism? And had they not received profound moral insights? Of course they had, for "happiness," as the chorus had revealed, "is wisdom" (1347). Not wealth, not power, not reason, not empire, not a strong navy, but wisdom. And, as the citizens applauded their own wisdom and moderation, they awarded Sophocles first prize for the *Antigone*; the popularity of the play caused the same audience to elect Sophocles general (*stratēgos*) in 441 BC along with his close friend Pericles, as Athens armed and prepared for the great conflict that its own tragic destiny urged upon them and that their own peculiar *hubris* made them lust after.

Notes

[1] Anthony Hecht and Helen H. Bacon, trans., *Seven Against Thebes* (New York: Oxford University Press, 1973), p. 29.

[2] Anne and Henry Paolucci, eds., *Hegel on Tragedy* (New York: Harper and Row, 1975), p. 178.

[3] Sophocles, fragment 583, trans. Bernard M. W. Knox, "The *Medea* of Euripides," *Oxford Readings in Greek Tragedy*, ed. Erich Segal (Oxford: Oxford University Press, 1988), p. 289.

[4] Paolucci, eds., *Hegel on Tragedy*, p. 325.

[5] A. J. A. Waldock, *Sophocles the Dramatist* (Cambridge: Cambridge University Press, 1951), pp. 49–79.

[6] Waldock, p. 52.

[7] Charles Segal, *Tragedy and Civilization: An Interpretation of Sophocles* (Cambridge, Mass.: Harvard University Press, 1981), pp. 179–88.

[8] Andrew Brown, ed. and trans., *Sophocles: Antigone* (Warminster, Wiltshire: Aris and Phillips, 1987). All translations cited from the play are from this edition.

[9] Brown, trans., p. 168.

[10] Mary R. Lefkowitz, *Heroines and Hysterics* (London: Duckworth, 1981), pp. 14–15. See also Goldhill, *Reading Greek Tragedy*, p. 102.

[11] Jean-Pierre Vernant and Pierre Vidal-Naquet, *Myth and Tragedy in Ancient Greece*, trans. Janet Lloyd (New York: Zone, 1990), p. 99.

[12] R. P. Winnington-Ingram, *Sophocles: An Interpretation* (Cambridge: Cambridge University Press, 1980), p. 128.

[13] Michelle Gellrich, *Tragedy and Theory: The Problem of Conflict since Aristotle* (Princeton: Princeton University Press, 1988), p. 55.

[14] Richard C. Jebb, ed., *The Antigone of Sophocles*, abridged ed. (Cambridge: Cambridge University Press, 1902), p. 182.

[15] Brown, trans., *Sophocles: Antigone*, p. 171.

Chapter Seven

"The Best of All Possible Wives": Euripides' *Alcestis*

> I should also speak of womanly virtues . . . great is the woman who is the least talked about among men, be it in praise or blame.
> Pericles, "The Funeral Oration"[1]

> A woman cannot despise the man beside her, without despising herself.
> Helen, *Helen*, 296-97[2]

Aeschylus' criticism of Euripides in the *Frogs*—that he undermined the Athenian educational system and the military establishment[3]—is the most overtly political legacy of any playwright before Ibsen. Euripides' relentless questioning of the values of the democratic patriarchy at least partly explains why he carried away the first prize only four times in his five decades of competition in the dramatic festivals. He placed more often third—that is last—than first. The ancient *Life of Euripides* puts it bluntly: "He was hated by the Athenians."[4] Tradition also tells us that an embittered and disillusioned Euripides spent his final years in self-imposed exile at the court of the King of Macedonia.

If his fellow citizens were largely blind to the merits of his plays, Athens' enemies apparently were not. The Athenian soldiers captured in the Sicilian expedition gained food and drink—some even their freedom—by singing verses of Euripides to their captors; likewise, the Spartans were said to have relented in their plans of razing the city of Athens at the end of the Peloponnesian War when the Athenians danced and sang the choruses of the *Electra*. The normally hard-hearted Spartans were moved to tears, and they could not bring themselves to destroy a city that had produced so great a poet. And Aristotle, even as he chided Euripides for his many weaknesses and structural problems, still conceded that he was "the most tragic of the poets."[5] Euripides would eventually triumph. He became the most popular and influential of all the Greek tragedians.

Euripides consciously manipulated and experimented with the form of tragedy much more than the other tragedians. He understood that form was not an abstract aesthetic principle but part of a work's meaning. Both Aeschylus' grand trilogic syntheses and Sophocles' relentless tragic closure had as much to do with politics and ideology as with structural principles. Tragic structure is questioned, violated, parodied, forced to the breaking point and turned inside out by Euripides. The distinctions between the genres themselves begin to blur. Sometimes only the thinnest pretense of form holds the Euripidean universe together.

Euripides also consciously exploited more than any other tragedian the power of emotion and sentiment in the drama. This is what Aristotle had in mind when he called him the "most tragic." Certainly, Aeschylus and Sophocles had realized the importance of emotional effect, and each created memorable scenes of overwhelming theatrical power. But none had overtly manipulated audience emotional response as ruthlessly and relentlessly as Euripides. Athenian audiences never knew quite what to expect from him.

Euripides is often linked with the sophists. As a youth, he attended the lectures of Protagoras, Anaxagoras and other major sophists. Tradition even tells us that the manuscript of Protagoras' explosive *On the Gods* was first read aloud in Euripides' home.[6] The sophists radically expanded the range of philosophical and ethical debate in Athens. Everything, including morality, religion and the state, now became subject to rational discourse and debate. Aeschylus had created a world where human action and divine guidance formed a coherent ethical cosmos. The gods had retreated and become more cryptic in the Sophoclean dramatic universe, but the ethos of Olympus still governed. In Euripides both human and divine worlds are emptied of moral and ethical signification, and the organic unity of the cosmos is shattered. Like Protagoras' lost philosophical work, *Contradictions*, Euripidean tragedy presents life as a mesh of insoluble contradictions.

The *Alcestis*, produced in 438 BC, has caused a bewildering array of critical responses. There is not even a consensus as to its genre: tragedy, comedy, romance, melodrama, tragi-comedy, satire, burlesque, parody or satyr play (with the drunken Herakles substituting for the traditional chorus of satyrs). At least as early as the third century BC, serious doubts about the play's status as "tragedy" had been raised. The great scholiast Aristophanes of Byzantium declared in his *Hypothesis* to the play:

> The drama is of the satyric kind [*saturikōteron*] in that it turns to joy and pleasure at the end, contrary to the tragic kind [*tragikon*]. The *Orestes* and the *Alcestis* are rejected from tragic poetry [*tragikēs poiēseōs*] in that they begin from disaster and end in joy and delight which belong rather to comedy [*cōmōidias*].[7]

The fact that it is the only known "tragedy" to have been produced as the fourth and final play in a tetralogy, where one would normally expect a satyr play, should explain some of the play's unusual qualities, especially as regards its tone and its satiric-comic elements.

In the *Alcestis*, another female title character exits to meet her death well before the end of the play. Alcestis is carried off after line 434, just one-third of the way into the play. As in Sophocles' *Antigone*, produced two years earlier, Alcestis is surrounded by a male chorus, and her function as protagonist is usurped by a male character. Both female characters are the objects, not the subjects, of their dramas. Both are dragged before the male audiences, not only to suffer and to provide aesthetic delight but also, as texts of the female, to be read, scanned and interpreted.

The *Alcestis* includes deities and heroes, but it is far removed from the Aeschylean-Sophoclean worlds of heroic mythology. Although set before a palace with gods, demi-gods and royalty as the main characters, the play actually takes place in front of the fifth-century home (*domos*) of a rather ordinary Athenian household (*oikos*). The word *domos* or *oikos* is used over sixty times in the play, and we even get a remarkably detailed portrait of the interior layout of the typical Athenian home. The traditional messengers have been replaced by maids or domestic servants. In this shrunken bourgeois-domestic environment, the possibilities for heroism or greatness are enormously reduced.

The *Alcestis* examines from a male perspective the three most important domestic relationships in the Athenian patriarchy: husband and wife, father and son, guest-friend and host. Each one of these patriarchal domestic institutions is threatened by the death of the wife/woman Alcestis, and healed by the return of the wife/woman to the household. The miraculous ending restores these relationships but not before the play has critiqued and satirized the social-sexual system. As William Arrowsmith puts it, "Euripides is dramatizing the incongruities of a culture—its received values against its actual or ideal values."[8]

Alcestis is ceaselessly praised as: "the very best of wives" (85), "by far the best of wives beneath the sun!" (151), "a woman by far the best of all" (442). She freely embraces her female role as victim. As a good wife—as indeed the best of all possible wives—Alcestis makes the ultimate wifely sacrifice. She goes from a symbolic nonentity to a literal nonentity. As the Serving Maid tells us: "How could any wife show more honor to her husband than by being willing to die for him?" (154–55). Alcestis, played by a male actor in drag, cuts a pitiable, if not a comic, figure. In her pathetic lamentations and threnodies of suffering, tragic stature is reduced to domestic pathos: "I see him there at the oars of his little boat in the lake, the ferryman of the dead, Charon with his hand upon the oar" (252–54).[9] Like Gaiev in *The Cherry Orchard*, Alcestis finds herself addressing speeches to the furniture:

> "O marriage bed,
> it was here that I undressed my maidenhood and gave myself up to this husband for whose sake I die.
> Goodbye...."
> (Lattimore, 176–79)

Just as Deianara had thrown herself on her marriage bed before she killed herself, Alcestis is provocatively sexualized. Perhaps the male audience flattered itself by imagining that the prospect of a woman's loss of sex with her husband was the greatest hardship that a wife about to die would face.

Alcestis, like a number of other females in Euripides—Iphigeneia and Polyxena for example—gains a semblance of tragic stature by taking upon herself the role of self-abnegating victim. In the context of the shrunken possibilities of the ordinary, middle-class world of the play, Alcestis becomes a kind of domestic, *bourgeois* Iphigeneia. Furthermore, Alcestis does what no woman could do in fifth-century Athens, and she attains what Greek women in real life could not even aspire to. She achieves the masculine virtues of honor and fame. Men sought honor (*aretē*) and won fame (*kleos*) in warfare and many other fields of endeavor, but a woman, as Pericles explained in his famous funeral oration honoring the Athenian war dead, because of "the standard which nature has set for your sex," could only win honor (*aretē*) by being anonymous, could achieve fame only by having no fame:

> Great is your glory [*aretē*] if you fall not below the standard which nature has set for your sex, and great also is hers of whom there is least talk among men whether in praise [*kleos*] or blame.[10]

Alcestis, like the male heroes of tragedy, is willing to die to defend her identity and the only ideal she can aspire to—indeed the only legal identity possible for a woman in fifth-century Athens—that of a wife/woman. She earns what Admetus calls her "good fame" or "fair renown" (*eukleēs*) (938).

The only heroism in the world of the play is shown by the title character, Alcestis, who is a female. But to the Athenian citizen audience, that a wife/woman could be brave was a literal contradiction in terms. Aristotle explains this in the *Politics*. In discussing the issue of slavery, "an institution both expedient and just" (1.2.15),[11] he asks the rhetorical question of whether it is possible for a slave to have virtues, such as wisdom (*sophrosunē*), courage (*andreia*) or justice (*dikaiosunē*) (1.5.4), adding:

> The same question could also be raised about the wife-woman and the child: do they also have virtues, and could a wife-woman be wise, brave and just . . .?[12]

Hath a woman wisdom, justice or bravery? The notion would have been inconceivable to the Athenian male, because "bravery" (*andreia*) meant literally "like a man" (man = *anēr, andros*):

> The wisdom of a wife/woman and that of a man are not the same, nor their courage and justice, . . . but the one is courage of command, and the other that of subservience, and the case is similar with the other virtues. (1.5.8)

Similarly in the *Poetics*, he points out that "bravery [*to andreian*] in a wife/woman is not proper."[13]

In his portrait of Admetus, Euripides zeroes in on the peculiar masculine gender *hubris* and male egocentrism at the center of the Athenian patriarchy. Admetus was the hero graced with the best of all possible wives—one who not only lived for him but died for him. In his version of the Alcestis text/myth, Euripides asks: What kind of man would allow someone else to die for him? Let alone expect it? What kind of man would behave this way? The answer, of course, is a man like any contemporary self-centered, smug Athenian citizen/husband. We may ask questions, but no characters in the play (except for his father) challenge Admetus. The generational rift between father and son in *Alcestis* is a precursor of the type of conflict that would later dominate new comedy. The most dramatic moment in the play is the stunning *agōn* between Admetus and his father:

> ADMETUS. At any rate, you most certainly surpass everyone in cowardice, seeing that, at the age you've reached, at the very end of your life, you weren't willing and didn't have the courage to die for your own son, but rather let this woman, no blood relation, do so. . . .
>
> PHERES. I sired you and brought you up to be the lord of this house but I owe you no obligation to die for you as well. . . . Don't do my dying for me and I won't for you! . . . And then you talk about *my* cowardice, when you, most base of all, were bested in courage by your wife, who died for you, the fine young husband!
> (641–98)

Pheres gives voice to the thoughts that at least some would have been thinking—that Admetus was not noble but a coward and hypocrite.

Euripides' Admetus may be overly hospitable to his guest-friends, but no one could accuse him of being overly sensitive to his wife. Throughout the play he is able to interpret events from his own point of view alone—all other perspectives are irrelevant. As she is about to die, he keeps interrupting Alcestis' emotional monody to tell her how much *he* is suffering (246–47, 250, 264–65, 273–74), reproaches her for abandoning him (391), and finally even convinces himself that he is suffering more than Alcestis: "I count my wife's lot happier than my own, though it seems not to be" (933–43). Leaping Hamlet-like onto her corpse, he vows to commission a life-size Alcestis doll to adorn his bed:

> A likeness of your person, fashioned by the skilled hands of a
> craftsman will be laid out on my bed. On this I'll fall and, as I
> embrace it, and call your name, although I'll seem to hold my dear
> wife in my arms, although I hold her not: a chill delight, I realize, but
> still I might in this way lighten the burden of my soul.
> (348–53)

Not only will Admetus suffer the loss of his faithful bedmate, but:

> The desolation within will drive me out again, when I look upon the
> marriage-bed with my wife no longer in it, and the chairs on which
> she used to sit . . . and dirty floors throughout the house;
> (943–47)

Poor Admetus, driven to despair by his empty bed and unwashed floors! Neither Euripides nor his audience was unaware of the masculine egocentricity and hypocrisy at the center of Ademtus' character. Euripides placed consistently last in tragic competitions not because he went over his audience's head but precisely because they saw all too well exactly what he was doing—critiquing the values of his culture and exposing the hypocrisy of its ideology.

However, Admetus has his defenders. Synnøve des Bouvrie states: "We have little evidence for thinking that the audience was supposed to react unfavorably to Admetos."[14] Anne Pippin Burnett also insists that Euripides did not intend Admetus to be seen as "a cad or a coward."[15] Viewed as a traditional protagonist, Admetus' *hamartia* would be his excess of hospitality. As the chorus puts it, "His noble nature is carried to an extreme of guest reverence." (600–1) The Servant also declares: "Far too guest-loving is that master mine!" (808)—Admetus just "can't say no" to a guest-friend. Admetus' "tragic flaw," his excessive hospitality, causes not only Alcestis' early death but also it ironically leads to the *peripeteia* that substitutes bliss for tragic pity and fear, joy for suffering.

If Admetus is a rather ordinary husband, an Athenian Torvald Helmer, the chorus clearly represents the average Athenian male point of view. Not only does the male chorus neither criticize nor find fault with Admetus, it outdoes him in heroizing the husband's pain and suffering at the loss of such a wife/woman. To both Ademtus and the chorus, Alcestis is not a person, she is a possession, a commodity—merely a wife/woman, a thing to be bought and sold, gained or lost. It would never occur to them that Alcestis, or any other wife/woman, could have a self. Thomas Rosenmeyer identifies this point of view as the distinguishing feature of the chorus in the play:

> Characteristic of the chorus as spotlighted by Euripides is their strong sense of masculine prerogative. . . . Alcestis must die, that is her obligation and her fate; any feeling that may be provoked by this fate is to be poured into sympathy with the lonely survivor. It is his loss, not hers, which feeds the compassion of the chorus. . . . The chorus, manly and middle-aged, . . . can speak and feel only with other men.[16]

Again and again the focus is deflected to what Admetus is feeling. The loss of Alcestis is a fate worse than his own death for Admetus (274), and the chorus fears that it may drive him to suicide (227–30).

The strange and ambiguous ending of the play further heightens the questions of genre, tone and interpretation. Some critics have tried to salvage a traditional tragic structure in the play, arguing that Admetus changes and has an *anagnorisis*, a "self-discovery"[17] or an "enlightenment as a result of a series of emotional shocks."[18] However, the text shows scant evidence of any change in character. Admetus ends the play exactly as he began it. He breaks each one of the vows he made to his dying wife. Ironically, he is apparently rewarded for his failings. His excessive hospitality saves him from ignominy, returns his wife from the grave and restores the *domos*.

But what are we to make of the veiled and mysteriously silent Alcestis at the end of the play? Euripides himself calls attention to her silence when he has Admetus ask: "Why does this wife of mine stand silent?" (1143). Herakles responds that she cannot speak "until she has been purified from consecration to the gods below and till the third day comes" (1145–47). What can this mean? Obviously, there was no Greek purification ritual for those who had risen from the dead. A. W. Verrall in his thought-provoking work on Euripides made the startling assertion that the whole death of Alcestis has been a ruse:

> There is no one now, and assuredly there was no one at Athens in the days of Protagoras, who *assuming these facts* would dream of a miraculous explanation, instead of the obvious explanation.[19]

Like Hermione in *The Winter's Tale*, he argued that Alcestis never actually died.

If we can assume that Alcestis has indeed actually died, several other possibilities exist. The fact that the veiled woman, whom we assume is Alcestis, does not speak could be explained by Euripides' apparent decision to make *Alcestis* a two-actor play.[20] The part of the veiled woman would have been played by a mute actor wearing a mask. We do not know why Euripides would have written a two-actor play at least two decades after three-actor plays were being produced,[21] but his early plays—such as *Medea*—are two-actor plays. By calling attention to the mute actor's inability to speak, Euripides for whatever reason would have been making an Athenian "in-joke"—the reason she can't speak is that it's a two-actor play.

But can we be so certain that the veiled and silent woman is Alcestis at all? Could not Herakles be forcing upon Admetus another wife/woman, a false Alcestis? As previously explained, "wife" and "woman" are the same word (*gunē*), and the Greek text contains no stage directions. The fact is that we are not exactly sure what is happening in the final moments of the play except that Admetus admits a veiled wife/woman into his household and bed chamber, clearly, by the way, recalling the Athenian marriage ceremony where the woman wore a veil. With Alcestis' body barely cold in the grave, is it possible that Admetus could break his vows to his dying wife and accept another wife/woman into his home and bed in order to please his guest-friend Herakles? The answer is yes. Despite critical efforts to create a new or "enlightened" Admetus, nothing that happens in the play suggests that Admetus has changed.

Is Admetus symbolically remarrying Alcestis or replacing her with another wife/woman, a false Alcestis? Euripides is teasing his audience with the silent woman. The playwright could make the silent woman (played by a man) speak at any moment—making it a three-actor play—and resolve all ambiguity, but he/she doesn't speak.

The point is that the veiled wife/woman is nothing more than a token exchanged by two men in the male-bonding ritual of guest-friendship. Even if the silent woman is actually Alcestis, she remains what she was at the beginning of the play—a *reductio ad absurdum* of the Periclean model of the nameless, faceless, silent wife/woman, a sign invented and defined by the male imagination. Cedric Whitman gives a more poetic and metaphysical explanation of Alcestis' silence: "The dramatic point of Alcestis' reticence is clear and effective: she has nothing to say.... The *Alcestis* is tragedy, tragedy of the Return from Death to Death in Life..."[22] In other words, Alcestis' tragedy is that she is forced to come back to "life" and return to her role of wife/woman.

The veiled woman may not be Alcestis, might not be Alcestis, need not be Alcestis. Admetus is an embarrassingly honest representative of the male egocentrism of his audience. When it comes to the wife/woman in his bed chamber, put a veil over her head and it doesn't quite matter who she is. One wife/woman is quite the same as another.

Notes

[1] Thucydides, 2.45.

[2] Robert Emmet Meagher, trans., *Euripides' Helen* (Amherst: University of Massachusetts Press, 1986), p. 21.

[3] *Frogs*, 1070–72. "You emptied the gymnasia, corrupted our youths with your lessons and taught the enlisted men how to argue with their officers."

[4] Mary R. Lefkowitz, *The Lives of the Greek Poets* (Baltimore: Johns Hopkins University Press, 1981), p. 167.

[5] *Poetics*, 1453a (28–30). Leon Golden, trans., *Aristotle's Poetics* (Englewood Cliffs, N.J.: Prentice-Hall, 1968), p. 22.

[6] T. B. L. Webster, *The Tragedies of Euripides* (London: Methuen, 1967), pp. 22–23.

[7] D. J. Conacher, trans., *Euripides' Alcestis* (Warminster, Wiltshire: Aris and Phillips, 1988), p. 63. Unless otherwise indicated, all translations from the *Alcestis* are from this parallel-text edition.

[8] William Arrowsmith, "'Conversion' in Euripides," *Twentieth Century Interpretations of Euripides' Alcestis*, ed. John R. Wilson (Englewood Cliffs, N.J.: Prentice-Hall, 1968), p. 34.

[9] Richmond Lattimore, trans., *Alcestis, The Complete Greek Tragedies: Euripides I*, eds. David Grene and Richmond Lattimore (Chicago: University of Chicago Press, 1955), p. 17.

[10] Thucydides, 2.45.2. Charles Forster Smith, trans., *Thucydides I* (Cambridge, Mass.: Harvard University Press, 1928), p. 341.

[11] H. Rackham, trans., *Aristotle: Politics* (Cambridge, Mass.: Harvard University Press, 1944), p. 25.

[12] *Politics*, 1.5.4. Unless otherwise noted, all translations from the *Politics* are my own literal version.

[13] *Poetics*, 1454a (23), my translation.

[14] Synnøve des Bouvrie, *Women in Greek Tragedy* (Oslo: Norwegian University Press, 1990), p. 198.

[15] Anne Pippin Burnett, "The Virtues of Admetus," *Greek Tragedy: Modern Essays in Criticism*, ed. Erich Segal (New York: Harper and Row, 1983), p. 254. Reissued in 1988 as *Oxford Readings in Greek Tragedy*.

[16] Thomas Rosenmeyer, *The Masks of Tragedy: Six Essays on Greek Dramas* (Austin: University of Texas Press, 1963), pp. 219–20.

[17] Webster, *The Tragedies of Euripides*, p. 52.

[18] D. M. Jones, "Euripides' *Alcestis*," *Twentieth Century Interpretations of Euripides' Alcestis*, ed. John R. Wilson., p. 60.

[19] A. W. Verrall, *Euripides the Rationalist* (Cambridge: Cambridge University Press, 1895), p. 76.

[20] First-actor: Apollo, Admetus, Servant; second-actor: Death, Maid, Alcestis, Pheres, Herakles. The child sings only a monody (393–403 and 406–415) which is at least partially corrupt and may be a later addition.

[21] For example the *Oresteia* was produced in 458 BC, twenty years before the *Alcestis*.

[22] Cedric H. Whitman, *Euripides and the Full Circle of Myth* (Cambridge, Mass.: Harvard University Press, 1974), p. 112.

Chapter Eight

Euripides' Everywoman: *Medea* and the Dramaturgy of Gender

> EURIPIDES.   The women are holding a general
>   Debate in the Temple to decide
>   How best to destroy me.
> MNESILOCHUS.   But why?
> EURIPIDES.   Because
>   They say I slander them in my plays.
>   Aristophanes, *Thesmophoriazusai*, 82–85[1]
>
> Go home now, and attend to your own work, the loom and
> the spindle. . . . War is men's business.
>   Hector to Andromache, *Iliad*, 6.490–92[2]

A culture is a social text composed of shared signs and values. Greek tragedies were imaginative dramatized readings of the social text of the Athenian democratic patriarchy through a formal civic discourse of dramatic actions, conventions and signs. Aeschylus and Sophocles had created metaphoric syntheses, dramatic resolutions and closure that reinforced and legitimized the dominant values, political mythology and gender ideology of the *polis*. Euripides intentionally sought to deconstruct or "misread" the idealized social text of the *polis* by exposing the perceived dominant ideology, usually represented as "reality" or the "real world," as false, gross and evil.

Euripides' misreading of the Athenian *polis* questioned its most privileged premise—masculine superiority and male moral-political self-righteousness. The males in Euripides' dramatic world are often infected with a pathological gender *hubris*. In the *Hecuba* and *Trojan Women*, for example, maleness is equated with brutalization and femaleness with victimization. Euripides creates an aesthetic world where women are brutalized on every level by men as part of their sexual-political identity. Both the victims and the victimizers are equally dehumanized.

What Aeschylus and Sophocles portrayed as reasonable or necessary are reduced in Euripides to rationalized sophistry; heroic aspiration is transformed to fanatical extremism. The idealized values and mythologized ideology of the democratic patriarchy had been asserted by Aeschylus and Sophocles with full seriousness. In Euripides the same values can only be expressed with ironic cynicism. In Sophocles concepts like justice had started to become ambiguous and contradictory. In Euripides all moral values are emptied of signification. Characters in the Euripidean universe have only a faint recollection of the time when justice or morality used to mean something.

Aristophanes accused Euripides of being a misogynist, claiming that he was slandering women by portraying them as vengeful, deceitful, baby-killing adulteresses. The charge of misogyny stuck until late-nineteenth- and early-twentieth-century feminists made Euripides' *Medea* a canonical text; feminist rallies in England and America often opened with readings of speeches from the *Medea*. Still, male critics earlier this century charged that "Euripides showed himself to be without pity for the vices and the transgressions of women,"[3] and, blithely unaware of the sexual nature of their metaphors, praised him in one category above all the other tragedians, namely that "Euripides penetrated still more deeply into the souls of women."[4] The notion that Euripides was a misogynist because he slandered women by exposing their characteristic faults is itself based upon misogynist assumptions.

In the *Thesmophoriazusai*, Aristophanes had Euripides' uncle dress-up in drag in order to sneak into the all-female festival. Aristophanes' real charge against Euripides, dramatically reinforced in the

Thesmophoriazusai, was obvious enough to his male audience—Euripides was a gender-turncoat. He had feminized tragedy, the most masculine institution of the Athenian democratic patriarchy, and symbolically castrated the manly, "lofty," heroic legacy of Aeschylus. Again and again, Euripides placed the female at the center of the action of his plays. What's more, this female perspective was dramatically privileged, not marginalized. Euripides' dramaturgy of gender startled and outraged Athenian audiences.

This is not to say that Euripides claimed to speak "for women" or that he was championing women's rights. The female is an invented, imaginative concept in Euripides no less than in Aeschylus or Sophocles, but he was intent on using gender to expose the flaws and failings of the Athenian social order rather than to reinforce the dominant ideology. The most densely complex and fully realized creations in Euripides are women—it is the males who are characteristically reduced to gender stereotypes and usually not very flattering ones.

The *Medea* is one of the most remarkable and important imaginative works in all of western literature. Here, Euripides invented a new version of the gender "female." Medea, "proud-hearted and not to be checked on her course"[5] (109), is presented in heroic terms, pursuing her own definition of herself, not simply an inversion or negative construct. Medea refuses to merely suffer and lament, to retreat to the background while male characters take over the action. She is initially encoded as an extreme sign of the "female as victim," but, as a non-Greek—a barbarian woman—she is able to strike back and pursue her revenge on a heroic scale. Medea is marginalized socially, culturally and politically. In many ways, she is the ultimate outsider, but the expected dramaturgy of gender is turned on its head. It is Jason's perspective that is marginalized and made dramaturgically "female." He is also made dramatically "female" by becoming a victim. From beginning to end, Euripides remained structurally committed to Medea as the central experience of the play, and he does not distance or subvert her point of view. As John Ferguson reminds us:

> It is impossible to overstress the power of Euripides' imagination in this identification with the woman's viewpoint—or the disturbing effect it must have had on the males in his fifth-century audience.[6]

The original audience response to *Medea* must have been outrage or bewilderment. The traditional masculine reading of the social text is presented not merely innocuously, or even satirically as in the *Alcestis*, but despicably. The play's point of view is so radical that some still contend that Jason was intended to be a sympathetic character.

Medea was performed in March 431 BC, a few months before the outbreak of the Peloponnesian War, a time of frenzied saber rattling and militarist jingoisms. With Athens preparing for war, before an audience of the soldiers and sailors and ephebes of Athens, imagine the shock when Medea declaimed, "I would rather fight three battles in the front lines than bear one child" (250–51).

Medea is not simply a woman; she is also an alien, doubly marginalized. She brings the perspective of the total outsider to the privileged Athenian male hegemonic discourse of tragedy. She turns this very alienation into a self and an identity. Medea despises the conventional gender stereotypes of women:

> You were born a woman
> And women though most helpless in doing good deeds,
> Are of every evil the cleverest of contrivers.
> (407–9)

At first glance, Medea might seem like another female constructed by inversion and/or negation, another axe-wielding, unnatural man/woman meant to conjure up male castration anxieties. Still Euripides passes no moral judgment upon her. In certain ways, she is closer to another symbolic child-slayer, Ibsen's Hedda Gabler, than to Clytemnestra or any other character in Greek tragedy. Just as Hedda struggles to prevent herself from becoming a pathetic heroine in a bourgeois, domestic well-made play, Medea is determined not to let herself become the traditional female victim in a Greek tragedy. She insists on her right to do what male protagonists have always done, indeed have been expected to do—to define herself and strive to become her vision of herself, regardless of law or morality. As the raging Achilles was Achilles or the foaming Ajax was Ajax, the outraged Medea will be Medea, not a simplistic inverse male or helpless female victim. And just as Hedda Gabler's actions baffle or are misread by the male-dominated cast of her play, Medea is an enigma to the representatives of the rigidly masculine gender-framework of the Corinthian/Athenian world of her play. Both characters refuse to play the parts that the masculine world order would force upon them; both are determined to write their own fates. But "People don't do such things!" Judge Brack tells us in his famous declaration at the end of *Hedda Gabler*. Jason is similarly aghast at the end of *Medea*—"No Greek wife/woman could do what she has done!" (1339) For both Ibsen and Euripides, this is precisely the point.

Medea has been a problem for critics at least as far back as Aristotle. As H. D. F. Kitto notes:

> The *Medea* is twice censured by Aristotle: the Aegeus scene is illogical and is not even used properly, and the end is artificial and therefore wrong. Moreover, by implication he condemns the murder of the children as "revolting" (*miaron*), and the catastrophe, the escape of Medea and the death of the innocent, is hardly what he approved.[7]

Aristotle tells us that the tragic protagonist should be good, at least more good than bad. Not a saint, not a villain, but someone like ourselves, so that we will be able to feel tragic pity. This character is led to his/her doom or catastrophe through some *hamartia*—a failing, error in judgment, mistake, sin or "missing of the mark."

Indeed, in the Aristotelean context, Euripides seemed to violate every principle of dramatic structure and characterization. First of all, Medea has no *hamartia*. She doesn't make any mistakes. Her plans succeed all too well. She doesn't miss the mark; she goes straight to it. Medea, unlike Ajax or Oedipus, intentionally commits her heinous crimes. She openly defies moral values, even the notion of morality itself, not by sophistic logic or hypocritical assumptions of superiority but as a response to the oppression and humiliation she has suffered. Her action also has fitting symbolic value, since she destroys Jason by striking at his dearest possessions, a man's two most valuable commodities in the patriarchal *polis*—his brand-new "legitimate wife" and his children (his potential heirs). Furthermore, in driving this stake in the heart of the patriarchy, Medea violates what, in terms of Athenian gender ideology, was assumed to be the most universal womanly value—the maternal instinct. Instead of protecting her children, she butchers them.

The play's ending refuses to simplify the conflict or the questions raised. Instead of healing the social sore he has exposed, Euripides pours acid on it. Helios' rescue of Medea denies the audience the opportunity of passing moral judgment upon her or of side-stepping the questions raised with the typical Aeschylean or Sophoclean choral platitudes. Hoisted in the crane above the male audience is this scowling, incomprehensible monster of a woman about to be whisked off to safety in, of all places, Athens! This final scene is crucial, because the *Medea* could still have been turned into a conventional, and morally uplifting, tragedy without it.

The *Medea* is even more structurally innovative than the *Alcestis*. Instead of placing dramatic obstacles in the path of the protagonist, Euripides does the opposite.[8] All the obstacles to Medea's revenge are removed so that she can race forward to more uncontrolled acts of rage. The ending is much more than a clever Euripidean paradox. All through the play, Euripides is leading the audience into an emotional trap that will spring on them and cause extreme moral anxiety. Initially, he creates sympathy for Medea as the suffering, "female" victim. Her outrage and resolve for vengeance are portrayed in heroic terms. Swept up in the fury of her emotional frenzy, we become dumbstruck as we watch Medea's retribution reach its full fury and savagery. We feel betrayed. The final moral insult is Medea's flight to safety on the *deus ex machina*. Euripides refuses to morally condemn or cast judgment on her. Medea is portrayed ultimately like a hurricane or a volcano—a force of nature to be reckoned with but not to be judged—and to whom moral categories like good and evil are irrelevant. The original audience certainly must have pulled back in revulsion at the ending and, if anything, felt pity for poor Jason.

Many critics have great difficulty in refraining from a moral judgment on Medea. Denys Page calls her "a witch," describing her revenge as "the inhuman cruelty of the child-murderess."[9] Objectively viewed, the crimes that Medea commits are no worse than the kinds of butchery committed by the great male heroes of tragedy and epic—Agamemnon, Orestes, Ajax, Achilles. The horrified response of some critics to her murder of her children is reminiscent of the outrage of nineteenth-century critics to Nora's abandonment of her children at the end of *A Doll House*. London's most influential critic Clement Scott called Nora "a mass of aggregate conceit and self-sufficiency" and railed against her because she "forgets her duty, forgets her very instinct as a mother, forgets the three innocent children . . . . forgets her responsibilities and does a thing that one of the lower animals would not do."[10] Like Nora, Medea insists upon the right to have a self-defined identity and to view the world the way the male characters do—as subject rather than object. Medea refuses to be reduced to a simple cipher in a male equation.

The Jason and Medea stories comprised one of the most popular cycle of legends in classical Greece. It was above all the great romantic love story—Jason and Medea were the Greek Romeo and Juliet. The major change Euripides made in the legend was Medea's murder of her children.[11] In one version of the myth, recorded by Pausanias, Medea was tricked into killing her children. As Denys Page explains:

> Zeus fell in love with her, but Medea refused him, to escape the wrath of Hera. In return, Hera promised to make her children immortal. . . . Medea exposed her children to some treatment which, instead of making them immortal, caused their death . . . Medea *unintentionally* killed her children.[12]

However, two other versions of the fate of the children were more prominent. A scholiast on Euripides records:

> The women of Corinth, impatient of obeying a foreign sorceress, rose against Medea and killed her seven sons and seven daughters.[13]

The Alexandrian commentator Didymus preserves the other version:

> Medea killed Kreon. Fearing the vengeance of his friends and kindred she fled to Athens. Her children, who were too young to accompany her, she deposited in the temple of Hera Akraia, where Kreon's kindred slew them, afterwards spreading a rumour that Medea killed her own children as well as Kreon.[14]

Euripides' version replaced the original story and became the best known.

Several characteristic dramaturgical possibilities for Medea would have presented themselves to the playwright. She could have been a passive suffering victim with no part in her children's deaths, or she could have killed her children or caused their death unintentionally or accidentally. He could have portrayed Jason heroically and made Medea a Clytemnestrian man-woman, obstinately opposing the rational values of male patriarchy. Instead Euripides made a startling choice. Medea would kill her children, not by accident but by choice. Furthermore, this horrifying action would be presented in heroic terms. Whatever the morality of Medea's actions, in the world of the play, she—a woman and a barbarian—is the only one capable of anything remotely resembling heroism. Euripides' revision of the myth was so shocking that the story circulated that Euripides had been bribed for political reasons by the Corinthians to make changes in the original version of the myth. However Euripides had his own reasons for making Medea kill her children, and needed no bribe from the Corinthians.

Before Euripides, Jason had been one of the great heroes of Greek mythology. Thirty years earlier, Pindar had used him to honor the victor of a chariot race in *Pythia 4*, praising Jason as "splendid beyond all others" (123).[15] Euripides, however, had a different purpose for his new Jason. He was especially acute in characterizing *hubristic* male egotism, and his Jason would be cut from the same cloth as Admetus had been. Admetus was egocentric, but he is sensitivity itself compared to Jason who declaims:

> But you women have got into such a state of mind
> That if your life at night is good you think you have
> Everything; but, if in that quarter things go wrong,
> You will consider your best and truest interests
> Most hateful.
>   (569–73)

He continues in this same vein the last time he sees Medea:

> You who have had the heart to raise a sword against
> Your children, you, their mother, and left me childless—
> You have done this . . .
> For the sake of pleasure in the bed you killed them.
> (1325–38)

Jason thinks that all Medea really wants is some good sex!

The character of Jason is a pointed attack on the values of the Athenian *polis*. He is so caught up in the language of personal gain and the logic of profit that he expects Medea to be impressed by his cleverness and thankful that she will now have a friend in high places, even hinting that someday she might become his mistress or concubine. The mythic scale and heroic aspirations of the earlier protagonists of Greek tragedy and epic have shrunk to Jason's pitiful declaration of his goals in life: "that we might live well, / And not be short of anything" (559–60). Although Medea is alienated legally and culturally, it is Jason who is alienated dramaturgically. Jason's perspective—the typical, rational, male Athenian—used to be the normative "choral" perspective of tragedy. Now it is not only discredited but also ridiculed. Jason is what the heroic Athenian male point of view has been reduced to—self-satisfied egotism, no longer concerned with morality but with comfort; not seeking justice but merely in preserving a thin veneer of "civilized behavior."

Through Medea Euripides gives voice to the suffering and rage of all the nameless and faceless oppressed of Athens:

> We women are the most oppressed creatures.
> Firstly, with an excess of wealth it is required
> For us to buy a husband and take for our bodies
> A master; for not to take one is even worse.
> And now the question is serious whether we take
> A good or bad one; for there is no easy escape
> For a woman, nor can she say no to her marriage.
> (231–37)

Euripides' Everywoman refuses to play the role of the pathetic, suffering victim. Instead, Euripides takes the notion of woman as radical "other" full circle and creates a new dramatic sign of the female. In *Medea* the traditional male hero (Jason) plays the traditional female role of victim; it is the victim who strikes out heroically. Medea, Euripides' Athenian Everywoman, could only aspire to a single identity—that of a wife. She loses even this tiny shred of an identity when Jason marries Creon's daughter. Medea has none of the traditional male options to regain her lost honor, such as personal combat with her foe or rushing headlong into battle. Everywoman had only one destiny and one fate—to marry and have children. When her honor—indeed her very identity—is taken from her, she strikes back at her oppressor with ruthless and unflinching amorality, using her children to exact pain for pain from her enemy:

> JASON. Oh, children I loved.
> MEDEA.   I loved them, you did not.
> JASON. You loved them, and killed them.
> MEDEA.   To make you feel pain.
>   (1397–98)

Medea strikes at the heart of the patriarchy, killing Jason's new "legitimate" wife and his progeny, seeking to destroy Jason's identity in the way he has destroyed hers. Here Medea acts within the exact parameters of the heroic code as Achilles had explained it: "giving pain to him that gives me pain" (*Iliad*, 9.615). When Medea says that she is "one who can hurt my enemies and help my friends" (809), she is explicitly referencing this central maxim of the heroic code.[16]

All of the Greek tragedians present a world of rigid gender polarity, where the male values of politics and the state oppose the female values of family and home. This gender conflict often throws the world into chaos. Aeschylus and especially Sophocles take us to the edge of the abyss, but it is always a carefully structured abyss. In Euripides the rupture does not heal, but it widens. No synthesis is possible, not even heroic defiance is any longer possible. Again and again, Euripides desperately lunges to sound the bottom notes of the anguish of the human experience in a universe devoid of moral signposts or ethical values.

Euripides intentionally misreads the social-sexual text to reveal its gaps, contradictions and absurdities. The male is not simply problematic in Euripides; it is pathological, debased and dehumanized. The tragedy of the Athenian *polis* is personified in Jason, the typical, well-heeled Athenian male who feels by nature superior to all other races, classes and sexes. Athens, like Jason, no longer dreams of great heroic deeds. With no more dragons to slay or golden fleece to pursue, the Athenian male now simply wants to live well, preserve the *status quo* and turn a good profit. Ironically, it is Medea, the alien, the outsider, the savage, the reviled Everywoman, who becomes the champion of individual rights. In a fitting Euripidean paradox, Medea butchers her children in order to affirm heroic values and the worth of the individual human being.

Notes

[1] Patric Dickinson, trans., *Aristophanes: Plays II* (London: Oxford University Press, 1970), pp. 132–33.

[2] My translation.

[3] Paul Decharme, *Euripides and the Spirit of the Times*, trans. James Loeb (New York: Macmillan, 1906), p. 111.

[4] Decharme, p. 101.

[5] Rex Warner, trans., *Medea, The Complete Greek Tragedies: Euripides I*, ed. David Grene and Richmond Lattimore (Chicago: University of Chicago Press, 1955), p. 63. All translations from *Medea* are from this edition.

[6] John Ferguson, *Euripides' Medea and Electra: A Companion to the Penguin Translation* (Bristol: Bristol Classical Press, 1987), p. 27.

[7] H. D. F. Kitto, *Greek Tragedy*, 3rd ed. (London: Methuen, 1978), p. 190.

[8] Kitto, pp. 190–202.

[9] Denys L. Page, ed., *Medea* (London: Oxford University Press, 1938), pp. xx–xxi.

[10] Michael Egan, ed., *Ibsen: The Critical Heritage* (London: Routledge, 1972), p. 114; *Theatre*, July 1889.

[11] For a full discussion of this question, see Emily A. McDermott, *Euripides' "Medea": The Incarnation of Disorder* (University Park: Pennsylvania State University Press, 1989), pp. 9–24.

[12] Page, *Medea*, p. xxiii.

[13] Page, p. xxiii.

[14] Page, p. xxiv.

[15] Richmond Lattimore, trans., *The Odes of Pindar*, 2nd ed. (Chicago: University of Chicago Press, 1976), p. 66.

[16] Elizabeth B. Bongie, "Heroic Elements in the *Medea* of Euripides," *Transactions of the American Philological Association* (1977), 107, pp. 27–56.

Chapter Nine

Resignation, Despair and the Great Capitulation: Sophocles' *Philoctetes*

> Individual success depends upon one's country.
> Euripides, *Philoctetes*, fragment 798 Nauck[1]
>
> Necessity is legislator here.
> Menelaus, *Orestes*, 486[2]

In 415 BC Athens expanded the Peloponnesian War with its boldest venture in the entire two-and-one-half decade conflict—the Sicilian expedition and the invasion of Syracuse. Thucydides recorded the debate at the assembly where Alcibiades swayed the masses with sophistic war-mongering oratory:

> It is necessary to plot against some and not let go our hold upon others, because there is a danger of coming ourselves under the empire of others, should we not ourselves hold empire over other peoples.[3] (6.8)

> The state, if she remains at peace, will, like anything else, wear herself out upon herself, and her skill in all pursuits will grow old; whereas, if she is continually at conflict, she will always be adding to her experience, and will acquire more, not in word, but in deed. (6.18)

The pro-war faction again carried the day, and : "*eros* afflicted them all alike to sail forth" (6.24). Athens now lusted after the war with an erotic intensity. Perhaps Thucydides recalled the "Hymn to *Eros*" from the *Antigone* (781-90) or, as F. M. Cornford suggested,[4] Clytemnestra's cautionary speech about the Trojan expedition in the *Agamemnon*:

> Only let no lust [*eros*] seize the army first,
> let no greed conquer them,
> to make them ravish what they should not.
> (341–43)[5]

Thucydides interrupts his normal passionless objectivity to interject:

> That in the seventeenth year after the first invasion of Attica they should have gone to Sicily, when already war-torn in all respects, and should have undertaken another war no whit less serious than that which was already being waged with the Peloponnesus—this, I say, was incredible. (7.28)

In June 415 BC, the armada with 30,000 men set sail. None would ever return. The reckless Sicilian expedition was the greatest disaster that would befall Athens. When news arrived of the destruction of the army and the fleet, including the large relief force, Athens plunged into political chaos. In 412 with much of Attica occupied by Spartan troops, and major Athenian allies and colonies in revolt, right-wing antidemocrats seized the moment to attack the democratic government. A Committee for public Safety was established and given emergency authority. The eighty-five-year-old Sophocles was called upon to serve his country once again as a member of this emergency committee (*proboulos*), in what Thucydides described as the greatest civic crisis ever to face the Athenian democracy.

In 411 BC, a right-wing *coup d'état* rid the city of even the pretense of democratic rule. The democracy was abolished outright and replaced by the oligarchy of "the Four Hundred." Radical democrats were rounded up and executed by right-wing death squads, as Thucydides baldly tells us, because the new government "thought it convenient to have them out of their way." He continues:

> Others they imprisoned, and also removed others from the city. Moreover, they made overtures to Agis, king of the Spartans, who was at Deceleia, saying that they wished to make peace and that it was only reasonable that he should be more ready to come to terms with them, having no longer to deal with the faithless democracy. (8.70)

The Athenian fleet and army at Samos, however mutinied and refused to recognize the oligarchic government. In the fall of 411 BC, the oligarchy of the Four Hundred was deposed and a new "government of the Five Thousand" was established in which "all who could furnish themselves with a hoplite's armor" (8.97) were granted citizen status. This new government, intended as a compromise between right-wing (oligarch) and left-wing (democrat) extremists, did not last long either. The rank-and-file sailors in the Athenian navy, whom Athens needed now more than ever, refused to fight for a government in which they no longer had the rights of citizenship. In April 410 BC, the democracy was reinstated.

With Attica occupied by Spartan troops, with Athens isolated and "instead of a city, a fort" (Thucydides, 7.28), with political terrorism tearing apart the fabric of the society—this was the context in which Sophocles sat down to write the *Philoctetes*, which was produced in the first City Dionysia after the restoration of the democracy in March 409 BC. He placed first for the eighteenth and last time. The *Philoctetes* is a deeply personal statement of both defiance and capitulation in which Sophocles attempts to sum up and synthesize the experience of fifth-century Athens in a final artistic testament. *Philoctetes* is the tragedy of a dying culture, Sophocles' swan-song of the Athenian democratic experience.

The eighty-seven-year-old playwright had seen Athens rise from the position of small city-state to the major power in the Greek world. He had seen the magnificent buildings on the Acropolis go up, the great leaders of the century come and go—he had even seen the democracy come and go. Indeed, he himself had played a major, possibly unwitting, role in the political events that had toppled the democracy.

Sophocles returned to a character that he had previously treated in *his Philoctetes at Troy*. The Philoctetes story was well-known, and at least five other playwrights, including Aeschylus and Euripides, dramatized the myth. Aeschylus had introduced the tradition of Odysseus' visit to the island to secure the return of Philoctetes and the famed bow of Herakles. Euripides' version, produced in 431 BC along with the *Medea*, had featured a rival embassy from the Trojans who sought to turn Philoctetes against his fellow

Greeks and aid the Trojans in the war.[6] Both had choruses of Lemnian islanders. The major innovations of Sophocles were the addition of the character of the young ephebe Neoptolemus and the *deus ex machina.* Sophocles also stressed the isolation of Philoctetes, making the island of Lemnos "uninhabited, untrodden by the foot of mortal man"[7] (line 2)—the very antithesis of the bustling, civilized community of the *polis.* Thus, there was no chorus of fellow islanders, instead a chorus of sailors, a fitting choice since the navy had become the mainstay of the democracy.

The play is filled with exotic and unusual images: a half-crazed Greek Robinson Crusoe stranded on a deserted island, a magical bow that never misses the mark, a mysterious wound that never heals. These elements, especially when viewed alongside the "happy" ending, almost suggest the world of romance rather than tragedy. However, the *Philoctetes* is not a retreat into escapist fantasy but a desperately personal tragedy, written in political shorthand and addressed directly to his fellow citizens amidst the contemporary civic crisis. It is unmatched in Sophocles for its relentless ideological discourse and its uncompromising examination of the moral-political premises of the Athenian democratic *polis*.

The *Philoctetes* is unusually visual.[8] The play includes many graphic and precise descriptions of objects and details, from Philoctetes' "bed of leaves pressed down as if somebody sleeps there" (33), his "crude wooden drinking-cup, the work of some poor craftsman" (35), "these rags . . . warming in the sun, full of some offensive matter from his sore" (38–39), and of course to the famous wound, with its foul stench and its oozing black puss: "a stream of blood from a burst vein has broken out darkly from his heel" (824–25).

The wound is not treated merely as an abstract symbol; it is as carefully described as a person might be. Despite the enormous pain it causes him, Philoctetes has developed a peculiar attachment to his wound. It is his personal badge of honor, the living symbol of his *aretē* and his devotion to the heroic code. It not only dominates his personality, it is part of his very identity, an emblem of the self, perhaps of tragic consciousness itself. Jan Kott insightfully compares Philoctetes to "Beckett's cripples,"[9] citing a line from *Waiting for Godot*: "We know we're alive because we suffer." This wound that will never heal destines Philoctetes to a life of howling and suffering, forever alone. Yet it is also Philoctetes' fate to be reintegrated into the human community and this most disgusting of outcasts to become the savior of the Greeks, just as the equally disgusting Oedipus will be similarly transformed in the *Oedipus at Colonus*.

The choice confronting Philoctetes, as framed by Sophocles, is unambiguous and clear-cut: personal honor (*aretē*) vs. the common good, morality vs. necessity, perhaps even freedom (*eleutheria*) vs. moderation (*sophrosunē*), the mottos of the left-wing and right-wing political parties.[10] Sophocles underscores this moral dilemma by his addition of the character of Neoptolemus, a young ephebe on the verge of manhood, the son of the very paragon of *aretē*, Achilles. Like Philoctetes Neoptolemus must make a crucial moral choice. He wants to become a man, to earn his *aretē* (lit. "manhood") and become a hero like his father. But to win this glory, he must commit an action of dishonor and treachery, betraying the very basis of the heroic code. Refusal means obscurity, a life with no fame—the very choice his father had rejected by sailing off to fight in the Trojan War—or disgrace before his comrades. Neoptolemus' youthful idealism confronts for the first time the workings of the real world, where political considerations are more important than morality, "Where the baser man proves stronger than the good, where goodness perishes and the coward rules" (456–57), as Philoctetes puts it.

Neoptolemus is an acute, sensitive portrait of an adolescent on the verge of manhood, facing an identity crisis. Unprepared, he finds himself an actor in a drama of deception, stage-managed and directed by the crafty Odysseus. He is presented with two roles models who represent diametrically opposed value systems. Philoctetes drives home this point, addressing the youth like a schoolboy: "You are not evil, but you have come, I think, after learning shameful lessons from evil men" (971–72).

The struggle for the bow of Herakles visually reinforces the play's conflict. Edmund Wilson compared it to Prospero's wand in *The Tempest*.[11] This bow has a famous history: Herakles had used it to cleanse the earth of savage monsters, thus making human civilization possible. Sophocles had earlier in his career dramatized the revenge of those bestial forces on the demi-god Herakles in the *Women of Trachis*. Additionally, the bow is used, as in the *Odyssey*, as a symbol of manhood and virility. When Philoctetes, in the throes of agony, entrusts it to Neoptolemus, this passing of the bow between the two men takes on ritual significance. Neoptolemus is transformed once he has touched the magical bow, not only embracing the cause of the aged hero but also reasserting the values of the outmoded heroic code, openly rejecting the treachery of Odysseus.

Odysseus is a far cry from the resourceful hero of Homer or Sophocles' earlier portrayal of the pious democrat in the *Ajax*. Odysseus, who had a special relationship with the goddess Athena and was thus imaginatively linked with Athens, was always known for his cleverness and pragmatism. However, the Odysseus of *Philoctetes* has now become a slick Athenian politician—"I am the man to fit the moment" (1049), he declares. Odysseus is as cynical a character as ever created by Sophocles—he is almost worthy of Euripides. Logic to him is mere sophistry, bravery mere foolishness, morality itself either stupidity or lack of the ability to compromise. He has no ideals left except victory; "It is my nature . . . always to win" (1052).

Odysseus tried to seduce Neoptolemus with visions of the glory he can win through a simple act of deception. With classic rationalization, Odysseus assures the lad that he can be as virtuous as he wants—tomorrow:

> I well know, boy, that it is not in your nature to tell lies
> like this, or to devise evil schemes.
> But bring yourself to do it, for a worthwhile victory is sweet to win.
> We will show ourselves as honorable men another day.
> *Now*, give yourself to me for a brief part-day of shamelessness,
> and then, for all remaining time,
> be called the most devout of mankind.
> (79–85)

"I prefer to fail by honor than to win by treachery" (94–95), the youth declares. Odysseus responds that his concern for morality is a sign of his youthful inexperience:

> I too, when I was young once,
> had a reluctant tongue but an active hand.
> (96–97)

Numerous ancient sources record that, as Athenaueus put it, "Sophocles was fond of young lads."[12] Does this inform Sophocles' dramatization of gender? *Philoctetes* is a uniquely masculine play, the only extant Greek tragedy without any female characters. The struggle of the two older men for the possession of the young adolescent male has strong homoerotic overtones. Carola Greengard notes: "The poetry of the play resonates with sexual language. Eroticized diction is used especially for the landscape and, even more surprisingly, for the hero's wound."[13]

The struggle for Neoptolemus becomes the fulcrum of the play's discourse and dramatic action. As much as the bow, he is fought over. He switches back and forth, reversing his decision several times, from reluctant acceptance of Odyssean necessity to finally joining the denial and isolation of Philoctetes. More than any other Sophoclean character, Neoptolemus seems to be free to choose his destiny. And yet, Sophocles and his audience knew the fate that ultimately awaited him. Neoptolemus, also known as Pyrrhus, dreams of winning fame as the hero of Troy. Instead, he is fated to be immortalized as the bloodthirsty butcher of Troy, as Shakespeare's portrait of him two thousand years later would still recall:

> Head to foot
> Now is he total gules, horridly trick'd
> With blood of fathers, mothers, daughters, sons,
> Bak'd and impasted with the parching streets,
> That lend a tyrannous and a damned light
> To their lord's murder. Roasted in wrath and fire;
> And thus o'ersized with coagulate gore,
> With eyes like carbuncles, the hellish Pyrrhus
> Old grandsire Priam seeks.
> (*Hamlet*, II, ii, 452–60)

The fate of the Greek army, however, and the famous bow rest in the hands of Philoctetes, and ultimately the action of the play turns on his decision. His choice, which could have been framed in numerous ways, is portrayed very specifically as one between honor and capitulation. The positive arguments for Odysseus' case are ignored by the playwright: the common good, patriotism, the suffering of the Greeks, the fate of his comrades, the end of the slaughter. Sophocles has totally deglorified the myth that even Euripides had employed to celebrate patriotism. The personal sufferings and agonies of Philoctetes are magnified and graphically presented, while the fate of his fellow Greeks are discounted or ignored. Philoctetes is the Sophoclean Prometheus. But the enemy is no longer the fascist on Mount Olympus or the Trojans on the battlefield but the politicians and self-serving demagogues like Odysseus inside the *polis*.

What is the meaning of manhood and virtue? What is the true cost of moral compromise? How long should Athens continue to place pragmatism over morality? Is a city where such logic rules worth saving? These are the questions being addressed in the political discourse of the play. Many exchanges must have echoed ones that had actually been heard in the assembly or on the streets of Athens:

> NEOPTOLEMUS. You do not think it shameful, then, to lie?
> ODYSSEUS. Not if the lie brings deliverance.
> (108–9)

While Philoctetes had spent a decade in isolation, the world had radically altered, and the rules of the game had changed. Victory was no longer the reward for self-sacrifice and heroism but, it seemed, for treachery and dishonor. Philoctetes is a time-traveler displaced in contemporary Athens, the last of an extinct species from the age when heroism and moral clarity still were believed to be possible. He refuses, totally and absolutely, to capitulate. He will not leave his hovel; he will not descend into the gross world of Odysseus; he will not negotiate with the ruling *junta* if the Atreïdae. He will remain alone and suffer, keeping alive the flame of the old heroic world—what Aeschylus might have called the "Spirit of Marathon"—even though its values seem to have become irrelevant.

The *Philoctetes* does not take place in the final year of the Trojan War, but in the closing years of the Peloponnesian War. In the Athens of 409 BC, heroism had become empty and hollow, and the difference between victory and destruction was no longer distinguishable. The spirit of compromise, personified by Aeschylus as Persuasion (*peithō*), had been replaced by inflexible ideological extremism—on both the right and the left. Right and wrong, moral and immoral, were now obsolete terms, all superseded by the new Odyssean *realpolitik*—the necessary or unnecessary. Odysseus was alive and well and living in Athens. Philoctetes decides to opt out of such a world. He will not bend to the will of the masses or the Atreïdae; he will not perform his "duty" or fulfill his historical destiny.

Edmund Wilson in his famous essay on the play interprets it as a parable of the artist's alienation from society. Artistic genius is inseparable from disease and disability. The artist suffers from what society considers a malodorous disease—artistic consciousness—and thus societies often expel or exile the artist from their midst. And yet, the artist has something that all desire—the magical bow of art and beauty. They want the beauty, but they do not want to tolerate the stench and puss that oozes from the artist's wound. Politicians, like Odysseus, want simply the bow—a bow which will serve the state. But society cannot have it both ways. If it wants the bow, it must also accept the sick person who wields If it.

The action of the *Philoctetes* reaches a total impasse, where no synthesis is possible in terms of the discourse of the play. The exiled Philoctetes totally rejects the claims of the *polis* and turns his back on necessity. He and his new comrade, Neoptolemus, will seek refuge from the cruel logic of history. This absolute refusal to compromise completes the tragic design of the play. Sophocles has gone as far as possible in terms of the human equation. Philoctetes is absolutely right in moral terms, and he will not capitulate; Odysseus is absolutely right in practical terms, and he will not relent.

At this moment, Sophocles introduces a perspective above and beyond the personal or merely human. We have been prepared for If it by the visual and dramatic prominence of the bow of Herakles. The human perspective is limited. Man can never find ultimate meanings in his own terms. Man is just a part of the equation; he is not finally "the measure of all things." As great as man is, in the face of the cosmos he is minuscule, and this is the central dramatic momentum of Sophoclean drama. The dramaturgical strategy of the ending of *Philoctetes* is the same as of that of Ibsen in *Little Eyolf*:

> RITA. Where should we look. Alfred—?
> ALLMERS (his eyes fixed on her). Upward.
> RITA (nodding in agreement). Yes, yes—upward.
> ALLMERS. Upward—toward the mountain peaks. Toward the stars. And toward the great silence.
> RITA (extending her hand to his). Thank you.[14]

For Sophocles, If it takes a *deus ex machina* to produce the same result.

Philoctetes retains his tragic stature and completes his action of refusal. But now he must resign himself to the will of the gods. he capitulates before a higher will and a higher power. Herakles tells him that he must accept history, accept the war and the slaughter, accept Odysseus and the Atreïdae, accept reality and his role, just as Sophocles had been forced to do. Even Philoctetes, the last of the heroes, must bend to necessity. He and Neoptolemus will go off as two comrades to Troy, not for personal glory or *aretē* but to be used by the state in the name of the common good.

The ending is almost Shavian in its complex and paradoxical irony. The wounded savage exile must rejoin the civilized but ruptured community of the *polis* so that both may be healed and saved. The moral innocence and spiritual energy of Youth, the rugged determination and aristocratic individualism of the Hero and the linguistic skills and technical prowess of Political Man must all somehow be reintegrated into the values of the communal and democratic *polis*. The Athenian citizenry—democrat and aristocrat—must pull together and find a new option, create a new synthesis. What was needed was what Aeschylus had achieved in the *Oresteia* a half-century earlier: a miracle of the imagination, an epiphany beyond the limited political perspective of the moment. Sophocles took upon himself the truly Herculean task of attempting to reachieve, remythologize and reenergize the poetics of Athenian democratic ideology in this most desperate environment.

The ending of *Philoctetes* is dramatically simple but politically and philosophically complex. Philoctetes is morally vindicated by his refusal to compromise. But Herakles imposes historical necessity upon him. Ironically, the cynical Odysseus is victorious. But Philoctetes will also be accepted back into the human community, and his wound will be healed. Herakles' promise to send Asclepius the healer to Troy reinforces the personal nature of this play for Sophocles. Sophocles of course was a priest in the cult of Asclepius. Philoctetes' final speech may have also been intended by the playwright as his formal farewell to his fellow citizens:

> Farewell Lemnos, sea-encircled,
> Blame me not but send me on my way
> with a fair voyage to where a great destiny
> carries me, and the judgement of friends and the all-conquering
> spirit who has brought this to pass.
>   (1464–68)[15]

Odysseus is not present because the actor who played him was now in the role of Herakles. Is Odysseus the man behind the mask of the god Herakles? I am not sure what, If anything, Greek audiences would have made of such doubling of roles. The playwright, however, who himself had introduced the third actor fifty years earlier, knew all too well that the same actor spoke from behind the masks of Odysseus and Herakles. Despite his desperate need to believe in the imaginative healing and spiritual rebirth of the *polis* through art, Sophocles knew that the future belonged to Odysseus.

Notes

[1] Translated by T. B. L. Webster, *The Tragedies of Euripides* (London: Methuen, 1967), p. 60.

[2]William Arrowsmith, trans., *Orestes, The Complete Greek Tragedies: Euripides IV*, eds. David Grene and Richmond Lattimore (Chicago: University of Chicago Press, 1958), p. 141.

[3]Thucydides, *History of the Peloponnesian War*, trans. Charles Forster Smith, 4 vols. (Cambridge: Harvard University Press, 1923). All citations from Thucydides are from this edition.

[4]Francis M. Cornford, *Thucydides Mythistoricus* (London: Oxford University Press, 1907), p. 214.

[5]Aeschylus, *The Oresteia*, trans. David Grene and Wendy O'Flaherty (Chicago: University of Chicago Press, 1989), p. 45.

[6]Webster, *The Tragedies of Euripides*, pp. 57-61, examines the known information on Euripides' *Philoctetes*.

[7]Sophocles, *Philoctetes*, ed. and trans. R. G. Ussher (Warminster, Wilts: Aris and Phillips, 1990). Unless noted, all citations from *Philoctetes* are keyed to the Greek text and employ this translation.

[8]Charles Segal, *Interpreting Greek Tragedy* (Ithaca: Cornell University Press, 1986), pp. 113–36, explores the visual aspects of Sophoclean tragedy.

[9]Jan Kott, *The Eating of the Gods*, trans. Boleslaw Taborski and Edward J. Czerwinski, 2nd ed. (Evanston, Illinois: Northwestern University Press, 1987), p. 169.

[10]W. Robert Connor, *Thucydides* (Princeton: Princeton University Press, 1984), p. 222.

[11]Edmund Wilson, "Philoctetes: The Wound and the Bow," *The Wound and the Bow* (Boston: Houghton Mifflin, 1941).

[12]Moses Hadas, *Ancilla to Classical Reading* (New York: Columbia University Press, 1954), p. 185, reviews the evidence on this matter.

[13]Carola Greengard, *Theatre in Crisis: Sophocles' Reconstruction of Genre and Politics in "Philoctetes"* (Amsterdam: Adolf M. Hakkert, 1987), p. 40.

[14]Henrik Ibsen, *The Complete Major Prose Plays*, trans. Rolf Fjelde (New York: Farrar, Straus, Giroux, 1978), pp. 935–36.

[15]David Grene, trans., *Philoctetes, The Complete Greek Tragedies: Sophocles II*, eds. David Grene and Richmond Lattimore (Chicago: University of Chicago Press, 1957), pp. 253–54.

Chapter Ten

Death Throes of the Patriarchy: Euripides' Final Plays

> This miserable woman [Helen] will die a miserable death as she deserves, and will inspire all women to be chaste.
> Menelaus, *Trojan Women*, 1055-57[1]

> On and on it goes, strangeness to strangeness succeeding, horror to horror.
> Chorus, *Orestes*, 1503-04[2]

In the year of Euripides' birth, Athens had saved Greece with their glorious victory at Salamis. The great Greek victories in the Persian wars and the miraculous *perepeteia* from catastrophe to triumph became central myths of the Athenian experience. Herodotus, the first Greek historian, structured his history of Greece as a grand Aeschylean drama culminating in a glorious theophany. Sometimes Herodotus' narrative seems that it would fit comfortably into the mouths of an Aeschylean or Sophoclean chorus:

> But one must look always at the end of everything—how it will come out finally. For to many the god has shown a glimpse of blessedness only to extirpate them in the end.[3]

In sharp and conscious contrast, Thucydides, the great historian of Euripides' generation, wrote his account of the history of the Peloponnesian War with grim objectivity. For both Aeschylus and Herodotus, history was a manifestation of the providential moral design of the universe. The Thucydidean universe, however, is amoral; one can say almost Euripidean. For both Thucydides and Euripides, the question was no longer "Can Athens save Greece?" but "Could Athens be saved from itself?"

With the destruction of the Sicilian expeditionary force, Athens experienced another great *perepeteia*—this time from patriotic euphoria to despair. The resulting political crisis—complete with terrorism and civil disobedience, assassinations and death squads, revolution and *coups d'état*—must have made the streets of the city resemble the scenes of a gruesome tragic drama.

Euripides' last four extant plays which can be securely dated—*Helen* (412), *Orestes* (408), *Iphigeneia at Aulis* (405) and the *Bakkhai* (405) bear witness to the last gasps of the collapsing Athenian social-cultural synthesis. In these plays, Euripides confronts the deepest anxieties and nightmares of the Athenian experience. The plot twists become more outrageous, the reversals more incredible, the theophanies more ironic and the resolutions more paradoxical. The most extreme sexual reversals and doubling of the female occur, and the body of the female becomes a frantic metaphoric battleground. Paradoxically, these works are both his most ferocious assaults on the values of the democratic patriarchy and a desperate attempt to reconfigure and save those very values. He even dares to imagine the destruction of the patriarchy itself, and he literally stages its dismemberment. The female is entirely reencoded and imaginatively empowered with almost mystical transcendence.

The *Helen*'s outrageous premise and protean action has made it another elusive work in the Euripidean canon. T. B. L. Webster cautions that "the *Helen* should not be taken too seriously,"[4] and to Gilbert Norwood, it defies all classification: "The drama is neither tragedy, nor melodrama, nor comedy, nor farce."[5] Recently, efforts have been made to position it as a problem play or "drama of ideas."[6] In general, however, critics and scholars are as bewildered as Menelaus: "I do not know what to make of it"[7] (496).

Instead of an ironic turn at the end of the story, here Euripides twists the premise. He ignores, indeed defies, the "accepted" or "true" version of the well-known myth of Helen which he himself had often employed and supplants it with an obscure version from the sixth-century poet Stesichorus. In the *Helen*, myth loses its stability, and history becomes fanciful ad hoc invention. Euripides does not simply question reality or blur the boundaries between truth and fiction; he discards perceived reality and transforms the false into the true, the dishonest into the honest, the promiscuous into the chaste.

Helen, even more than her half-sister Clytemnestra, was the most reviled and denigrated figure in Greek literature, especially in tragedy. The Peloponnesian War only heightened the hostile attitudes toward both of these Spartan women. Euripides had previously shown little sympathy for this icon of female promiscuity: three years earlier he had presented a rather negative Helen in the *Trojan Women* (415 BC). In the *Helen*, however, Euripides seems to recant and say to his audience: everything that you have ever heard about Helen, the great whore, is false; the woman who left her husband, Menelaus, and shared the bed of Paris, causing the Trojan War, was not really Helen at all, but a fake Helen, a phantasm, an illusion, a "clone"; the "real Helen" had actually spent the Trojan War in Egypt, chaste and faithful, pining for her husband.

In the context of the Athenian political crisis, certain metaphoric, if not allegorical, aspects of the play would have been immediately apparent. Menelaus' sea-tossed wanderings and ragged state obviously would have recalled the doomed Sicilian expedition. As Robert Meagher explains:

> For the original audience of Euripides' *Helen*, absorbing the aftershocks of Sicily, there could have been little ambiguity regarding the real identity of Troy or "the greatest Armada in history," . . . Sicily, Empire, Helen: they are all one.[8]

Athens too had been living a fantasy life where truth and fiction, the moral and the immoral, had been inverted. It had embraced a phantom and was now on the verge of total destruction. Athens could be saved not by another grand military venture nor another political fantasy but only by reexamining the morality of its collapsing ideology and exchanging the false back for the true.

Helen is almost Pirandellian, and the play could be called *Two Helens in Search of a Self*. Its dramatic action, complications and plot twists raise many significant philosophical and aesthetic questions. At the center of the play is the theme of metamorphosis and the literal struggle for control of the body of Helen, the archetype of female sexuality.

The struggle for the possession of Helen's body by the two kings, Menelaus and Theoclymenus, is a battle to define the central institution of the Athenian *polis*—patriarchal marriage, which depended upon control of the body of the woman through female chastity and female marital fidelity. Through its incredible premise, its miraculous *anagnorisis* and cleverly contrived *perepeteia*, Euripides trades one archetype for another; the chaste and virtuous wife supplants the promiscuous, unfaithful whore. To accomplish this, he clones Helen and splits her into two.

Menelaus and Theoclymenus both want Helen as wife. Theoclymenus, an Egyptian imaginatively descended from Aeschylus' Egypt, threatens to take her by force. Menelaus wins her back, not merely as a sexual object or a commodity but as a companion, almost a comrade-in-arms. Helen successfully navigates between the two contradictory worlds and achieves this trope of impossibility. The play ends with the reunion of the husband with the "true" wife, and the "false" Helen vanishes. The two lovers sail off into the sunset, presumably to life happily-ever-after. The ending not only rehabilitates Helen's image, it also reencodes female sexuality in an attempt to restore moral authority to the debased and masculinized ideology of the *polis*. Menelaus too is reconfigured. He is not the petty, craven cuckold one has grown to expect. The coward becomes a hero; the whore becomes a virtuous wife.

While Helen's beauty stands as a metaphor for art, the princess Theonoë's prophetic skills are evidence of the mystical powers of the feminine that have been imaginatively excluded from Athenian culture and society. The play establishes and examines a complex dialectical mesh of antitheses, the most obvious of which is the false and true Helen, but also includes the world of Egypt and the world of Troy, the struggle between feminine life-sustaining values and masculine life-destroying ones, the idealized embodiment of the feminine world-spirit in the sensuous realm of Art (Helen) and the spiritual realm of Religion (Theonoë).[9] The two major male figures—Menelaus and Theoclymenus—likewise represent two extremes of masculinity. Theoclymenus wants to possess Helen as an object, and he doesn't care if he has to use force. Menelaus has become the sensitive husband who accepts his wife as a partner.

Helen can be read as a metaphor for art or language, both of which create illusions and invent fake "realities." The *Helen* presents a world where anything can happen, where values, indeed reality itself, have lost their stability, where things can turn into their opposites with almost whimsical abandon. Amidst this seeming chaos, the concept of masculinity is redefined, a new sign of female sexuality is empowered, and a central institution of the *polis* (marriage) is miraculously restored and validated.

Euripides opened his *Orestes* at the City Dionysia in March 408 BC with the following:

> There is no form of anguish with a name—
> no suffering, no fate, no fall
> inflicted by heaven, however terrible—
> whose tortures human nature could not bear
> or might not have to bear.
>   (*Orestes*, 1–5)

Plutarch tells us that Socrates stood up in the Theatre of Dionysus and asked that these lines be repeated. From Aristophanes of Byzantium's declaration over two thousand years ago that "its ethics are dreadful"[10] to William Arrowsmith's description of it as "distorted by a bitterness so pervasive that it seems at times almost gratuitous,"[11] *Orestes* has always seemed particularly nihilistic, even for Euripides. In the final rewriting of the classic Oresteian legend, he strips away the mantra of justice from the story and reduces it to a shameless battle for sexual-political power.

Euripides' Orestes and Electra are far removed from the heroic offspring of Aeschylus. Orestes is mentally deranged, described again and again as an animal, while Electra stalks around "as good as dead" [*isonekues*] (200), "groaning, lamenting, weeping in the night" (207).[12]

Mythology once again collides with the reality of contemporary Athens. The matricides do not waste their efforts with pious appeals to morality. When pressed by Menelaus about Apollo's "unjust and immoral order" (417), Orestes' answer echoes the Athenians' arrogant response in the Melian dialogue as he declares: "We obey the gods—whoever the gods may be" (418).

Euripides presents Orestes, Electra and Pylades, not as heroic defenders of justice, not even as deluded but self-righteous transgressors but as a gang of political thugs and terrorists, "juvenile delinquents of a startlingly modern depravity,"[13] as B. M. W. Knox puts it. In fifth-century Athens, Frank Nisetich notes, audiences would have noted "a troubling similarity" between the young comrades and those "who had played the role of assassins in the oligarchic seizure of the government in 411 BC."[14] Orestes and Pylades are portrayed as radical antidemocratic aristocrats.

Orestes also is a foaming idealogue of male supremacy who has read and memorized his Aeschylus:

> My father begot me,
> my mother gave me birth. She was the furrow
> in which his seed was sown. But, without the father,
> there is no birth. This being so, I thought,
> I ought to stand by him, the true agent
> of my birth and being, rather than with her
> who merely brought me up.
>   (552–57)

His speech before the people's assembly—which he holds in contempt—is a naked and shameless appeal to extremist gender ideology:

> Men of Argos, . . . it was for your sake
> as much as for my father that I killed my mother. . . .
> you might as well go kill yourselves right now
> or accept the domination of your women.
>   (932–37)

The assembly of the people, which constantly buzzes around in the background and margins of the play, votes death for the matricides.

Reminiscent of Thucydides' narration of the shameless amorality that dominated debates in the Athenian assembly during the later years of the war, the Messenger explains that the vote went against them because: "Orestes' example was dangerous for parents" (893). He also informs them that an extremist faction in the city still supports their cause:

> What had he done,
> after all, but avenge his father's murder
> by killing a godless, worthless, adulterous woman?
> A woman, what was more, who kept men from war,
> kept them at home, tormented by the fear
> that if they left, those who stayed behind
> would seduce their wives....
> (924–29)

Female sexuality and the encoding of gender has become extremely complex and problematic. Two virgins (Electra and Hermione) are matched against two unfaithful wives (Clytemnestra and Helen). The real crime of Clytemnestra is the same as Helen's—adulterous sexuality. In the House of Atreus, not only have marital relations been debased but also all familial ties have become threatened. Although the characters of Greek tragedy should not be submitted to Freudian psychoanalysis, it is difficult to view the attachment of brother and sister in this play as merely filial. When it appears that she and Orestes may be killed, Electra cries:

> If only one sword
> could kill us both! If we could only share
> one coffin together.
> (1051–53)

Killing Clytemnestra is no longer enough. The gender terrorists next turn to Helen, the archetype of uncontrolled female sexuality. "Death to Helen!" [*Helenēn phoneuein*] (1130) becomes their battle cry:

> Mark my words, Orestes.
> There will be bonfires and celebrations in Argos;
> men will call down blessings on our heads,
> thank us, congratulate us for doing away

> with a vicious, worthless woman. No longer
> shall they call you "the man who murdered his mother."
> No, a fairer title awaits you now,
> the better name of "the killer of Helen
> who killed so many men."
> (1136–44)

Helen displaces Clytemnestra as the object of the trio's vilifications. For Orestes, killing his mother was only the first step because, as he puts it: "I can never have my fill of killing whores" [*tas kakas*] (1590). Electra has an almost orgasmic release when she hears Helen cry out in pain:

> ELECTRA. *Murder!*
>   *Butcher!*
>   *Kill!*
> Thrust your twin swords home!
> Slash, now slash again!
> Run the traitress through,
> kill the whore who killed
> so many brave young men. . . .
> (1301–5)

Hermione—the Periclean woman revisited—is a counter-type of the female, an anti-Helen, bleached of all sexuality. Holding a knife to her throat, the terrorists seize her as a hostage and begin to torch the palace. The god Apollo must intervene to reimpose order.

The object of the conflict in the *Orestes* is the female sexuality. Once again there is a literal struggle for Helen's body. Both the family unit (husband/wife, brother/sister, mother/daughter-son, uncle/nephew-niece) and the *polis* itself are threatened with disintegration. The *Orestes* dramatizes the dissolution and restoration of the institution of the family, albeit heavily laced with irony. The women in the play are all rescued and rehabilitated. The great whore, Helen, is whisked off to heaven and resurrected as a goddess. The two virgins are married off. By these transactions and manipulations, the family structure of the patriarchy and the transition of generations is accomplished. Again, the female substitutions that Euripides makes are significant—death is exchanged for deification, corrupted sexuality for celestial purity (Helen), innocence for marriage (Hermione) and radical obsessive virginity for marriage (Electra).

Euripides died in 406 BC in Macedonia, but the following year he would be a central figure on the Athenian stage: a character in Aristophanes' *Frogs* in January 405 and as the author of the posthumously produced *Iphigeneia at Aulis* and *Bakkhai* at the City Dionysia in March 405, the final City Dionysia before the surrender of the city. The citizens of Athens awarded the deceased Euripides the first prize that they had denied him so many times during his lifetime.

In *Iphigeneia at Aulis*, Euripides asks the question "can the Trojan War be stopped?" The answer is no. Each character in the play attempts to stop the murder of the innocent Iphigeneia and to prevent the war, but to no avail. Once again, the play is marked by a breathtaking series of reversals and a fantastic *deus ex machina*.

The play opens with possibly the most rapid sequence of reversals in extant Greek tragedy, beginning with Agamemnon's decision to spare Iphigeneia. After an *agōn* with his brother, Menelaus also reverses his demand for Iphigeneia's death, only to find Agamemnon's fear of the vengeance of the Greek army has caused Agamemnon to waver once again and decide to kill his daughter. Clytemnestra, when she learns of the planned sacrifice, begs the aid of Achilles, who agrees to stand beside Iphigeneia and protect her. After all this, Iphigeneia is not to be spared, and the war is not to be stopped. In an astonishing reversal, Iphigeneia chooses her own death and freely sacrifices herself for the cause of Greece.

Once again, Euripides gives Helen a key symbolic part in the drama. Although she never appears on stage, from Agamemnon's first monologue in the prologue (49–87) she is central. Again and again, that "wicked wife" [*kakon lekhos*] (389), "O wicked Helen" [*ō tlēmon Helenē*] (1253), is identified as the cause of the war and the troubles and is compared to the spotless, virginal Iphigeneia, who must pay the price for Helen's infamy:

And so our child,
In her beauty, you pay as price for a woman
Of evil. So you buy with our best beloved

> A creature most loathed and hated.[15]
> (1168–71)

Agamemnon must choose between the masculine values of war and the feminine values of life, the male civic interests of the state and the female domestic values of the home and the family. Euripides duplicates this dilemma in Achilles' betrothal to Iphigeneia, and he must similarly choose. The males in the world of the *Iphigeneia in Aulis* are not even "man enough" to be grossly evil; they are disgustingly petty and craven. Agamemnon finally decides to kill his daughter because he is a coward; Achilles decides to defend her, not for moral or ethical reasons but to defend his ruffled masculine pride:

> Now must I tell you, it is not on account
> Of this marriage I have said these things—
> No—there are many girls for marrying,
> But I cannot endure the insult and injury
> Which Lord Agamemnon has heaped upon me!
> (958–61)

Achilles' sensitive manly *aretē* has been violated because he has been deceived. The democracy is no longer the heroically idealized system as portrayed by Aeschylus. Democratic values have devolved to mob rule—all fear the blood-thirsty off-stage masses whom Odysseus, the demagogue, has whipped into a mad frenzy demanding Iphigeneia's death:

> AGAMEMNON.   He is cunning
>   In his tactics always and his ear
>   Is close to the mob. . . . with these words
>   Will he arouse and seize the very soul
>   Of the army, order them to kill you
>   And me—and sacrifice the girl.
>   (526–33)

As Clytemnestra maneuvers to save her daughter and Achilles prepares to go to his death defending her (and his honor), Iphigeneia suddenly changes her mind in an extraordinary speech:

> It is hard to hold out against the inevitable. . . .
> Now mother, listen to the conclusion
> that I have reached. I have made up my mind to die.
> I want to come to it
> with glory, I want to have thrown off
> all weak and base thoughts, Mother,
> look at it with my eyes,
> and see how right I am. . . .
> Because of me, Greece
> will be free, and my name will be blessed there.
> (1369–80)[16]

The only nobility in *Iphigeneia at Aulis* is shown by socially marginalized characters. The motives of the free-born males are all revealed as base and craven in the end, even Achilles, who was normally portrayed as a paragon of masculine virtue and heroism.

Patriotism, however, is not the sole reason for Iphigeneia's choice:

> There is another thing. It would not
> be right for this man
> to join battle with the whole of the army
> and die for the sake of a woman.
> If it means that one man can see the sunlight
> what are the lives of thousands of women
> in the balance?
> (1393–99, Merwin and Dimock)

It is not surprising that Achilles replies: "What you have said is beautiful and worthy of your country" (1407–8, Merwin and Dimock). Iphigeneia's *peripeteia* conveniently not only saves Greece, but it redeems the male world and removes the stain of moral guilt from the male characters. By making her sacrifice a freely chosen action, no one can be blamed. No less than Alcestis, Iphigeneia chooses death in order to save the male. Iphigeneia achieves her tragic trope of impossibility, the union of the right and the necessary.

To freely choose what is necessary. As Achilles puts it: "You have reconciled what should be with what must be" (1408–9, Merwin and Dimock). Has Iphigeneia been won over by the war propaganda, or is she heroically sacrificing herself? Her reasons are a *reductio ad absurdum* of Athenian gender ideology: (a) the life of a single man is worth more than thousands of women, and (b) it is wrong to allow men to die for the sake of a mere woman. Ironically, the Greeks are preparing to do exactly that by waging war on account of Helen. Iphigeneia wants herself—not Helen—to be "the face that launched a thousand ships."

The figure of Helen casts a long shadow over the action. Menelaus asks his brother: "But what has Helen / To do with this girl of yours?" (493–94). He receives no answer, but she has everything to do with Helen. The male ritual of warfare demands the symbolic sacrifice of the body of the unstained female. Iphigeneia embraces the expiational role of anti-Helen, the virginal, scapegoat that men will exchange for the great promiscuous whore.

Structural and dramatic order is restored by Iphigeneia's act of self-sacrifice, but our text does not end there. Once again, an exchange of female signs has occurred. The female archetype of sexuality and lust has been exchanged for the chaste virginal one. Here, yet another substitution is made. At the moment the sword falls, Iphigeneia is whisked away from the altar by Artemis and a deer put in her place. The goddess Artemis turns this final act of violation into pure ritual by substituting the deer for the body of the female. This also evokes the ritual of Dionysus, where an animal was substituted for the god, and thematically links the play to the *Bakkhai*, which was part of the same trilogy.

The *Iphigeneia at Aulis* is not a deathbed conversion of Euripides to jingoistic macho patriotism. Iphigeneia does not simply die for the state, she dies a fanatic, embracing the crazed masculine bloodlust of the army. The Greeks want a martyr, so she plays the part of martyr to the hilt:

> I am coming bringing salvation for Greece,
> and victory. Lead me.
> (2004–5)

No ethics are left. No morality is left. No free will is left. Whatever sacrifice the war demands is necessary and will occur. In this logic of fanaticism, "feelings" such as morality are extravagant and selfish. In a final and brutal irony, we cannot be sure whether the Messenger's account, backed up by Agamemnon, is true or just the latest and most brilliant version of propagandistic Atreus-speak. Euripides has created an aesthetic version of the Athens that he fled, a nihilistic universe where only crimes or meaningless gestures are possible. Iphigeneia's self-sacrifice is not heroism; it is a gesture in a void. This ironic and cynical reversal is all that is left for Euripides—possibly it is his response to Sophocles *Philoctetes*, produced shortly before he had left Athens as an exile.

The *Bakkhai* retells one of the oldest stories of tragedy and includes another ritual sacrifice where a substitution takes place. In the *Iphigeneia at Aulis*, an animal was substituted for a human; in the *Bakkhai*, a human (Pentheus) is substituted for an animal. Euripides returns to what he believed to be the original myth of tragedy as his final testament. In the *Bakkhai*, Dionysus, the patron saint of drama, comes back for one last fling. "I'm back" [*hēkō*],[17] he declares to open the play. In grand poetry, exotic rhythms, romantic coloring and choral grandeur, Euripides will challenge Aeschylus himself. In simplicity of structure and form, he will attempt to out-Sophocles Sophocles.

The *Bakkhai* dramatizes a conflict over the meaning of gender and sexuality. Gender is rigidified in the Penthean state but blurred by Dionysus and his worshipers. In this final apotheosis of Greek tragedy, Pentheus will travel full circle. His reversal scene is the most famous, total and terrifying *perepeteia* in Greek tragedy. Before our eyes, he is transformed from disbeliever to celebrant, from man to woman. In his preparation for the Dionysian ritual of ecstasy, Pentheus also reenacts the preparation of an actor for the Dionysian ritual of theatre—he changes his sex by donning the clothing and exaggerated mannerisms of the female. The cross-gender performances in tragedy have also affected the god—he has now been feminized to the point of androgyny.

Not only the family, the state and the meaning of sexuality are at stake in the *Bakkhai* but also the legitimacy of the godhead himself. The conflicts between man and nature, the rational and the irrational, reason and passion, the male and the female all converge and are resolved in the radical democratized godhead Dionysus. This play captures both the irresistible lure of and revulsion at this mystical Dionysian spirit. The Penthean state can only be maintained by rigid gender polarity, which the presence of Dionysus threatens. Athenian gender ideology has allowed man to build cities as well as culture and civilization, but it now threatens that very culture with annihilation.

What is a human being? Is man closer to god or closer to beast? Is the male or the female more important? Instead of the Apollonian defense of the patriarchy, the answer of *Bakkhai* is the paradox embodied in the god Dionysus. Dionysus is not a man nor a woman—he is man/woman. He is also a man/beast and rational/irrational. Civilization cannot comprehend this essential paradox. Rulers cannot legislate him away or imprison him; philosophers cannot explain or understand him.

Pentheus is Athenian political/philosophical man. He is the purest and most extreme example of the rationalist point of view toward religion and the gods. He is not a sophist or a hypocrite, but he is still an unmistakable product of the urban *polis*, proud and self-confident in his maleness and the civilization built upon it. The *Bakkhai* presents a confrontation between Greek rationalism at its most sophisticated and Greek wisdom at its most terrifying.

As Aphrodite did to Hippolytus, Dionysus makes a simple but absolute demand of Pentheus: worship me! This he refuses to do, but he, nevertheless, finds himself part of the Dionysian rituals of *sparagmos* (tearing apart of the sacrificial animal) and *omophagia* (eating the animal's raw flesh), a celebration not where he eats but is eaten. Like the Athenian *polis*, Pentheus has sought to deny and repress an essential component of the human being. He views the feminized Dionysus as his antithesis, not the part of himself that he actually is—by denying Dionysus' divinity, he also seeks to deny that they are born of the same mother, Semele.

Pentheus is finally turned inside out, and the Dionysian ritual is gruesomely celebrated. The chorus goes from sadness to joy (when Dionysus liberates himself from prison) and then from ecstasy to horror.

There is no reconciliation at the end between god and man, man and nature, male and female. The mother has killed and mutilated her son. The Dionysian ritual of rebirth and fertility becomes one of death and destruction. Pentheus is offered neither a life-affirming choice nor an act of defiance. No act of refusal remains. Euripides has deconstructed the social-sexual text into complete and absolute paradox. Rational synthesis or logical understanding is no longer possible.

At least in the world of Aeschylus and Sophocles, we knew what a man was and what a woman was and what a god was. Even in Euripides' *Hippolytus* written two decades earlier, sexuality may have been extreme, but it was at least stable. Hippolytus and Theseus remained in their pathologically male environment, and Phaedra stuck to her female domain and womanly ways. In the *Bakkhai*, the boundaries of gender and sexuality totally blur. In an instant, Pentheus, the spokesman for male rationalism, is turned into a drag queen worrying about his makeup and the hem of his skirt. This moment was probably particularly terrifying, but certainly not without its edge of dark humor, to its audience. In this moment, Euripides dramatizes and visualizes the ultimate Athenian male psycho-sexual nightmare—not women behaving like men, not even men behaving like women but the dissolution of masculinity itself. Not only is the patriarchal order of the *polis* disrupted, but the body of the male monarch is dismembered by crazed women.

Shortly after the production of the *Bakkhai* and the *Iphigeneia at Aulis*, the Athenians suffered their final defeat at Aegospotomi. The Spartan army closed their stranglehold around the city, Athens surrendered and was occupied. On the stage of history, the city of Athens acted out the *Bakkhai* not the *Oresteia*. The desperate Athenians sang and danced the choral odes from Euripides' *Electra*. The Spartan soldiers were so moved that they decided not to burn the city. However, at Spartan spear point, the democracy was abolished. The reign of terror of the Thirty Tyrants followed. Hundreds of radical democrats were rounded up and given swift "revolutionary justice."

The Athenians eventually overthrew the Thirty Tyrants. They also re-established a stable democratic government based on solid middle-class values. They even regained some of their power and influence in the Greek world until Macedonia abolished the democracy. Although Spartan torches did not burn her physically, Athens had been gutted spiritually. With the waning of the radical democracy, tragedy lost its political and aesthetic moment. The much safer and more easily controlled form of philosophy succeeded tragedy as the central forum of civic discourse. The comfortable and providentially controlled world of new comedy replaced the blasphemy, obscenity and political questioning of old comedy. Within a few decades, by the middle of the fourth century, Greek tragedies had gone the way of the legends they were based upon—they were myths of a vanished era.

Notes

[1] Shirley A. Barlow, ed. and trans., *Euripides' Trojan Women* (Warminster, Wiltshire: Aris and Phillips, 1986), p. 133.

[2] William Arrowsmith, trans., *Orestes, The Complete Greek Tragedies: Euripides IV*, eds. David Grene and Richmond Lattimore (Chicago: University of Chicago Press, 1958) p. 195. All translations from the *Orestes* are from this edition.

[3] Herodotus, 1.32. David Grene, trans., *The History: Herodotus* (Chicago: University of Chicago Press, 1987), p. 48.

[4] T. B .L. Webster, *The Tragedies of Euripides* (London: Methuen, 1967), p. 201.

[5] Gilbert Norwood, *Greek Tragedy* (New York: Hill and Wang, 1967), p. 262.

[6] Cedric H. Whitman, *Euripides and the Full Circle of Myth* (Cambridge, Mass.: Harvard University Press, 1974), p. 68.

[7] Richmond Lattimore, trans., *Helen, The Complete Greek Tragedies: Euripides II*, eds. David Grene and Richmond Lattimore (Chicago: University of Chicago Press, 1958), pp. 210–11. All translations from the *Helen* are from this edition.

[8] Robert Emmet Meagher, *Helen: Myth, Legend and the Culture of Misogyny* (New York: Continuum, 1995), pp. 107–8.

[9] See Charles Segal, *Interpreting Greek Tragedy: Myth, Poetry, Text* (Ithaca: Cornell University Press, 1986), pp. 222–267.

[10] Aristophanes of Byzantium, *Hypothesis*. M. L. West, ed. and trans., *Euripides: Orestes* (Warminster, Wiltshire: Aris and Phillips, 1987), p. 61.

[11] William Arrowsmith, "Introduction to *Orestes*," *The Complete Greek Tragedies: Euripides IV*, eds. David Grene and Richmond Lattimore (Chicago: University of Chicago Press, 1958), p. 106.

[12] M. L. West, trans., *Euripides: Orestes*, p. 75.

[13] P. E. Easterling and B. M. W. Knox, eds., *The Cambridge History of Classical Literature*, Vol. I, Part 2 (Cambridge: Cambridge University Press, 1989), p. 79.

[14] John Peck and Frank Nisetich, trans., *Euripides' Orestes* (Oxford: Oxford University Press, 1995), p. 12.

[15] Charles R. Walker, trans., *Iphigenia in Aulis*, *The Complete Greek Tragedies: Euripides IV*, eds. David Grene and Richmond Lattimore (Chicago: University of Chicago Press, 1958), p. 277. All translations from the *Iphigenia in Aulis* are from this edition unless otherwise noted.

[16] W. S. Merwin and George E. Dimock, Jr., trans., *Euripides' Iphigeneia at Aulis* (New York: Oxford University Press, 1978), pp. 85–86.

[17] Robert Bagg, trans., *The Bakkhai* (Amherst: University of Massachusetts Press, 1978), p. 19.

Bibliography

A Guide For Further Reading

This is not a traditional bibliography but a list of publications that should be useful or interesting for further study in the areas treated in this book. It includes works that I have found provocative or enlightening.

Reference and Background
Amos, H. D., and A. G. P. Lang. *These Were the Greeks*. 1979.
Boardman, John, and others, eds. *The Oxford History of the Classical World*. 1986.
Brown, Andrew. *A New Companion to Greek Tragedy*. 1983.
Csapo, Eric, and William J. Slater, eds. *The Context of Ancient Drama*. 1995.
Diehle, Albrecht. *A History of Greek Literature from Homer to the Hellenistic Period*. 1994.
Easterling, P. E. *The Cambridge Companion to Greek Tragedy*. 1997.
Ferguson, John. *A Companion to Greek Tragedy*. 1972.
Hadas, Moses. *Ancilla to Classical Reading*. 1954.
Harsh, Philip W. *A Handbook of Classical Drama*. 1944.
Harvey, Paul. *The Oxford Companion to Classical Literature*. 1st ed. 1937.
Hornblower, Simon, and Anthony Spawforth, eds. *The Oxford Classical Dictionary*. 3rd ed. 1997.
Howatson, M. C., ed. *The Oxford Companion to Classical Literature*. 2nd ed. 1989.
Lefkowitz, Mary R. *The Lives of the Greek Poets*. 1981.
Talbert, Richard J. A. *Atlas of Classical History*. 1985.

Mythology, Ritual and Religion
Bremmer, J. N. *Greek Religion. Greece and Rome: New Surveys in the Classics*. 1994.
Burkert, Walter. *Ancient Mystery Cults*. 1987.
———. *Greek Religion*. 1985.
———. *Homo Necans: The Anthropology of Ancient Greek Sacrificial Ritual and Myth*. 1983.
———. *Structure and History in Greek Mythology and Ritual*. 1979.
Cornford, Francis Macdonald. *From Religion to Philosophy*. 1912.
Dodds, E. R. *The Greeks and the Irrational*. 1951.
Easterling, P. E., and J. V. Muir, eds. *Greek Religion and Society*. 1985.
Harrison, Jane Ellen. *Epilegomena to the Study of Greek Religion*. 1921.
———. *Prolegomena to the Study of Greek Religion*. 1903.
———. *Themis: A Study of the Social Origins of Greek Religion*. 1912. 2nd ed. 1927.
Hesiod. *Theogony. Hesiod and Theognis*. Ed. Dorothea Wender. 1973.

Kurtz, D. C., and J. Boardman. *Greek Burial Customs*. 1971.
Nilsson, Martin P. *Greek Folk Religion*. 1961.
Otto, Walter F. *Dionysus: Myth and Cult*. 1995.
Parke, H. W. *Festivals of the Athenians*. 1977.
Parker, Robert. *Athenian Religion: A History*. 1996.
Polignac, François de. *Cults, Territory and the Origins of the Greek City-State*. 1995.
Simpson, Michael, trans. *Gods and Heroes of the Greeks: The Library of Apollodorus*. 1976.
Thomson, George. *Studies in Ancient Greek Society*. 1949.
Tyrrell, William Blake, and Frieda S. Brown. *Athenian Myths and Institutions: Words in Action*. 1991.
Vernant, Jean-Pierre. *Mortals and Immortals: Collected Essays*. 1991.
Walker, Henry John. *Theseus and Athens*. 1995.
Zaidman, Louise B., and Pauline S. Pantel. *Religion in the Ancient Greek City*. 1992.

Origins of Tragedy

Alexiou, M. *The Ritual Lament in Greek Tradition*. 1974.
Cornford, Francis Macdonald. *The Origins of Attic Comedy*. 1914.
Else, Gerald F. *The Origin and Early Form of Greek Tragedy*. 1965.
Gaster, Theodor H. *Thespis: Ritual, Myth and Drama in the Ancient Near East*. 1950. 2nd ed. 1977.
Herington, John. *Poetry into Drama: Early Tragedy and the Greek Poetic Tradition*. 1985.
Kirby, E. T. *Ur Drama: The Origins of Theatre*. 1975.
Murray, Gilbert. "Excursus on the Ritual Forms Preserved in Greek Tragedy." Appendix to Jane Ellen Harrison, *Themis*. 1912.
Pickard-Cambridge, Arthur. *Dithyramb, Tragedy and Comedy*. 1927. 2nd ed. Rev. T. B. L. Webster. 1962.
Ridgeway, William. *The Origins of Tragedy*. 1910.
Schlesinger, A. C. *Boundaries of Dionysus: Athenian Foundations for the Theory of Tragedy*. 1963.
Silk, M. S., ed. and trans. *Nietzsche on Tragedy*. 1981.

History, Politics, Sociology and Ethnography

Aristotle. *The Athenian Constitution*. Trans. P. J. Rhodes. 1984.
Aristotle. *Politics*. Trans. Ernest Barker. Rev. R. F. Stalley. 1995.
Beye, Charles Rowan. *Ancient Greek Literature and Society*. 1987.
Burnell, Martin. *Black Athena: The Afro-Asiatic Roots of Western Civilization*. Vol. I: *The Fabrication of Ancient Greece*. 1987.
Cartledge, Paul. *The Greeks: A Portrait of Self and Others*. 1993.
Connor, W. R. *The New Politicians of Fifth-Century Athens*. 1971.
Davies, J. K. *Wealth and the Power of Wealth in Classical Athens*. 1981.
Georges, P. *Barbarian Asia and the Greek Experience*. 1994.
Grene, David, trans. *Herodotus: The History*. 1987.
Hatzfield, Jean. *History of Ancient Greece*. Rev. André Aymard. 1966.
Jaeger, Werner. *Paideia: The Ideals of Greek Culture*. Vol. I. 2nd ed. 1945.
Kagan, Donald. *The Archidamian War*. 1974.
_____. *The Fall of the Athenian Empire*. 1987.
_____. *The Outbreak of the Peloponnesian War*. 1969.

_____. *The Peace of Nicias and the Sicilian Expedition.* 1981.
_____. *Pericles and the Birth of Athenian Democracy.* 1991.
Lacey, W. K. *The Family in Classical Greece.* 1968.
Lambert, S. D. *The Phratries of Attica.* 1994.
Little, Alan M. G. *Myth and Society in Attic Drama.* 1942. Rpt. 1967.
Loraux, Nicole. *The Invention of Athens: The Funeral Oration in the Classical City.* 1986.
Mattingly, H. B. *The Athenian Empire Restored: Epigraphic and Historical Studies.* 1996.
Ober, Josiah. *Mass and Elite in Democratic Athens.* 1989.
Plutarch. *The Rise and Fall of Athens.* Trans. Ian Scott-Kilvert. 1960.
Powell, Anton. *Athens and Sparta: Constructing Greek Political and Social History from 478 B.C.* 1988.
Rhodes, P. J. *The Greek City States: A Sourcebook.* 1986.
Romilly, Jacqueline de. *The Great Sophists in Periclean Athens.* 1992.
Ste. Croix, G. E. M. de. *The Class Struggle in the Ancient Greek World.* 1981.
Sealy, Raphael. *The Athenian Republic.* 1987.
Sinclair, R. K. *Democracy and Participation in Athens.* 1988.
Slater, Philip E. *The Glory of Hera: Greek Mythology and the Greek Family.* 1971.
Snowden, Jr., Frank M. *Before Color Prejudice.* 1983.
_____. *Blacks in Antiquity.* 1970.
Stanton, G. R. *Athenian Politics c. 800–500 BC: A Sourcebook.* 1990.
Starr, Chester G. *The Ancient Greeks.* 1971.
Stockton, David. *The Classical Athenian Democracy.* 1990.
Thucydides. *History of the Peloponnesian War.* Trans. C. F. Smith. 4 vols. 1919–23.
Vernant, Jean-Pierre. *Myth and Society in Ancient Greece.* 1990.
Vidal-Naquet, Pierre. *The Black Hunter: Forms of Thought and Forms of Society in the Greek World.* 1986.
Whitehead, D. *The Ideology of the Athenian Metic.* 1977.

Gender and Sexuality

Bassi, Karen. *Acting Like Men: Gender, Drama, and Nostalgia in Ancient Greece.* 1998.
Blundell, Sue. *Women in Ancient Greece.* 1995.
Cameron, A., and A. Kuhrt. *Images of Women in Antiquity.* 1983.
Cantarella, Eva. *Bisexuality in the Ancient World.* 1992.
_____. *Pandora's Daughters.* 1987.
Coward, Rosalind. *Patriarchal Precedents: Sexuality and Social Relations.* 1983.
Dolan, Jill. *The Feminist Spectator as Critic.* 1988.
Dover, K. J. *Greek Homosexuality.* 2nd ed. 1989.
Evans, Arthur. *The God of Ecstasy: Sex-Roles and the Madness of Dionysus.* 1988.
Fantham, Elaine, and others, eds. *Women in the Classical World: Image and Text.* 1994.
Halperin, David M. *One Hundred Years of Homosexuality and Other Essays on Greek Love.* 1989.
_____, and others, eds. *Before Sexuality: The Construction of Erotic Experience in the Ancient Greek World.* 1989.
Johns, Catherine. *Sex or Symbol: Erotic Images of Greece and Rome.* 1982.
Just, Roger. *Women in Athenian Law and Life.* 1989.
Keuls, Eva. *The Reign of the Phallus: Sexual Politics in Ancient Athens.* 2nd ed. 1993.

Lefkowitz, Mary R. *Heroines and Hysterics.* 1981.
_____. *Women in Greek Myth.* 1986.
_____, and Maureen B. Fast, eds. *Women's Life in Greece and Rome.* 1992.
Loraux, Nicole. *The Children of Athena: Athenian Ideas About Citizenship and the Division Between the Sexes.* 1993.
_____. *The Experiences of Tiresias: The Feminine and the Greek Man.* 1995.
Nussbaum, Martha C. *Love's Knowledge: Essays on Philosophy and Literature.* 1990.
Paglia, Camille. *Sexual Personae: Art and Decadence from Nefertiti to Emily Dickinson.* 1990.
Peradetto, J., and J. P. Sullivan, eds. *Women in the Ancient World.* 1984.
Pomeroy, Sarah B. *Goddesses, Whores, Wives and Slaves.* 1975.
Reeder, Ellen D., ed. *Pandora: Women in Classical Greece.* 1996.
Richlin, Amy, ed. *Pornography and Representation in Greece and Rome.* 1992.
Schaps, D. M. *Economic Rights of Women in Ancient Greece.* 1979.
Sealy, Raphael. *Women and Law in Classical Greece.* 1990.
Sissa, Giulia. *Greek Virginity.* 1990.
Spretnack, Charlene. *Lost Goddesses of Early Greece.* 1978.
Strauss, Barry S. *Fathers and Sons in Athens: Ideology and Society in the Era of the Peloponnesian War.* 1993.
Tyrrell, William Blake. *Amazons: A Study in Athenian Myth-Making.* 1984.
Winkler, John J. *The Constraints of Desire: The Anthropology of Sex and Gender in Ancient Greece.* 1990.
Wright, F. A. *Feminism in Greek Literature: From Homer to Aristotle.* 1923.

Theatre History

Arnott, Peter D. *Public and Performance in the Greek Theatre.* 1989.
Bieber, Margarete. *The History of the Greek and Roman Theatre.* 1939.
Donaldson, John William. *The Theatre of the Greeks: A Treatise on the History and Exhibition of the Greek Drama.* 7th ed. 1860. Rpt. 1973.
Easterling, P. E., and B. M. W. Knox. *Cambridge History of Classical Literature.* Vol. I, Part 2. 1989.
Edmunds, Lowell, and Robert W. Wallace, eds. *Poet, Public and Performance in Ancient Greece.* 1997.
Flickinger, Roy C. *The Greek Theatre and Its Drama.* 4th ed. 1960.
Garner, Richard. *From Homer to Tragedy.* 1990.
Goff, Barbara, ed. *History, Tragedy, Theory: Dialogues on Athenian Drama.* 1995.
Green, J. R. *Theatre in Ancient Greek Society.* 1994.
Haigh, A. E. *The Attic Theatre.* 3rd ed. 1907.
_____. *The Tragic Drama of the Greeks.* 1903.
Hammond, N. G. L. *The Conditions of Production to the Death of Aeschylus.* 1972.
Pickard-Cambridge, Arthur. *The Theatre of Dionysus in Athens.* 1946.
_____. *The Dramatic Festivals of Athens.* 2nd rev. ed. 1988.
Taplin, Oliver. *Greek Tragedy in Action.* 1978.
Walcot, P. *Greek Drama in Its Theatrical and Social Context.* 1976.
Walton, Michael J. *Greek Theatre Practice.* 1980.
Webster, T. B. L. *Greek Theatre Production.* 2nd ed. 1970.

Critical Works on Greek Tragedy

Alford, C. Fred. *The Psychoanalytic Theory of Greek Tragedy.* 1992.
Aristotle. *Poetics.* Trans. Gerald F. Else. 1967.
Bouvrie, Synnøve des. *Women in Greek Tragedy.* 1990.
Brendan, Christopher, and Reginald Pelling, eds. *Greek Tragedy and the Ancient Historian.* 1996.
Euben, J. Peter, ed. *Greek Tragedy and Political Theory.* 1986.
Gellrich, Michelle. *Tragedy and Theory.* 1988.
Girard, René. *The Violence and the Sacred.* 1977.
Goldhill, Simon. *Reading Greek Tragedy.* 1986.
Hall, Edith M. *Inventing the Barbarians: Greek Self-Definition Through Tragedy.* 1990.
Heath, M. *The Poetics of Greek Tragedy.* 1986.
Jones, John. *On Aristotle and Greek Tragedy.* 1962.
Kaufmann, Walter. *Tragedy and Philosophy.* 1968.
Kitto, H. D. F. *Greek Tragedy.* 3rd ed. 1978.
Knox, Bernard M. W. *Word and Action: Essays on Ancient Theatre.* 1986.
Kott, Jan. *The Eating of the Gods.* 1974.
Lattimore, Richmond. *The Poetry of Greek Tragedy.* 1958.
Lesky, Albin. *Greek Tragedy.* 3rd ed. 1978.
Lloyd-Jones, Hugh. *Greek Epic, Lyric, and Tragedy.* 1991.
Loraux, Nicole. *Tragic Ways of Killing a Woman.* 1987.
Lucas, D. W. *The Greek Tragic Poets.* 1959.
McAuslan, Ian, and Peter Walcot, eds. *Greek Tragedy.* 1993.
Meier, Christian. *The Political Art of Greek Tragedy.* 1993.
Mikalson, Jon D. *Honor Thy Gods: Popular Religion in Greek Tragedy.* 1991.
Mills, Sophie. *Theseus, Tragedy and the Athenian Empire.* 1997.
Norwood, Gilbert. *Greek Tragedy.* 1967.
Nussbaum, Martha C. *The Fragility of Goodness: Luck and Ethics in Greek Tragedy and Philosophy.* 1986.
Padel, R. *In and Out of the Mind: Greek Images of the Tragic Self.* 1992.
Paolucci, Anne, and Henry Paolucci, eds. *Hegel on Tragedy.* 1975.
Porter, David H. *Only Connect: Three Studies in Greek Tragedy.* 1987.
Rehm, Rush. *Marriage to Death: The Conflation of Wedding and Funeral Rituals in Greek Tragedy.* 1994.
Rhodes, Norman L. *Ibsen and Greek Tragedy.* 1996.
Romilly, Jacqueline de. *Time in Greek Tragedy.* 1968.
Rosenmayer, Thomas G. *The Masks of Tragedy.* 1963. Rpt. 1971.
Scodel, Ruth, ed. *Theatre and Society in the Classical World.* 1993.
Seaford, Richard. *Reciprocity and Ritual: Homer and Tragedy in the Developing City-State.* 1994.
Segal, Charles. *Interpreting Greek Tragedy: Myth, Poetry, Text.* 1986.
Segal, Erich, ed. *Oxford Readings in Greek Tragedy.* 1988.
Silk, M. S., ed. *Tragedy and the Tragic: Greek Theatre and Beyond.* 1996.
Stanford, W. B. *Greek Tragedy and the Emotions.* 1983.
Vernant, Jean-Pierre, and Pierre Vidal-Naquet. *Myth and Tragedy in Ancient Greece.* 1990.
Vickers, Brian. *Towards Greek Tragedy: Drama, Myth, Society.* 1973.
Winkler, John, and Froma Zeitlin, eds. *Nothing To Do with Dionysos?: Athenian Drama in Its Social*

Context. 1990.
Yale Classical Studies. 25. *Greek Tragedy.* 1977.
Young, Sherman P. *The Women of Greek Drama.* 1953.

Critical Studies of Aeschylus

Bloom, Harold, ed. *The Oresteia. Modern Critical Interpretations.* 1988.
Conacher, D. J. *Aeschylus: The Earlier Plays and Related Studies.* 1996.
_____. *Aeschylus' Oresteia: A Literary Commentary.* 1987.
_____. *Aeschylus' Prometheus Bound: A Literary Commentary.* 1980.
Dodds, E. R. *Morals and Politics in the Oresteia.* 1973.
Gagarin, Michael. *Aeschylean Drama.* 1976.
Goldhill, Simon. *Aeschylus: The Oresteia. Cambridge Landmarks of Literature.* 1992.
_____. *Language, Sexuality, Narrative: The Oresteia.* 1984.
Herington, John. *Aeschylus.* 1986.
Hogan, James C. *A Commentary on the Complete Greek Tragedies: Aeschylus.* 1984.
Kuhns, R. *The House, The City and The Judge.* 1962.
Lebeck, Ann. *The Oresteia: A Study in Language and Structure.* 1971.
McCall, M. H., ed. *Aeschylus: A Collection of Critical Essays.* 1972.
Murray, Gilbert. *Aeschylus, the Creator of Tragedy.* 1940.
Podlecki, Anthony J. *The Political Background of Aeschylean Tragedy.* 1966.
Rosenmeyer, Thomas G. *The Art of Aeschylus.* 1982.
Smyth, H. Weir. *Aeschylean Tragedy.* 1924.
Taplin, Oliver P. *The Stagecraft of Aeschylus.* 1977.
Thomson, George. *Aeschylus and Athens.* 3rd ed. 1968.
Winnington-Ingram, R. P. *Studies in Aeschylus.* 1983.

Aeschylus: Recommended Translations and Commentaries

Burian, Peter, trans. *The Suppliants.* 1991.
Dawson, Christopher M., trans. and comm. *The Seven Against Thebes.* 1970.
Fagles, R., trans., and W. B. Stanford, comm. *The Oresteia.* 1975.
Fraenkel, Eduard, ed. and comm. *Agamemnon.* 3 vols. 1950.
Grene, David, trans. *Prometheus Bound.* 1942.
_____. trans. *Seven Against Thebes.* 1956.
_____, and Wendy O'Flaherty, trans. *The Oresteia.* 1989.
Hall, Edith, ed., trans. and comm. *Persians.* 1996.
Havelock, Eric A., trans. and comm. *Prometheus Bound.* 1970.
Hecht, Anthony, and Helen H. Bacon, trans. *Seven Against Thebes.* 1973.
Lattimore, Richmond, trans. *Oresteia.* University of Chicago. 1953.
Lembke, Janet, trans. and comm. *Suppliants.* Oxford. 1975.
_____, and C. J. Herington, trans. and comm. *Persians.* 1981.
Lloyd-Jones, Hugh, trans. and comm. *Agamemnon.* 1970. Rpt. 1979.
_____, trans. and comm. *Eumenides.* 1970. Rpt. 1979.
_____, trans. and comm. *The Libation Bearers.* 1970. Rpt. 1979.
_____, trans. and comm. *The Oresteia.* 1994.

Podlecki, Anthony J., trans. and comm. *Eumenides*. 1989.
_____, trans. and comm. *The Persians*. 2nd ed. 1991.
Scully, James, and C. J. Herington, trans. and comm. *Prometheus Bound*. 1975.

Critical Studies of Sophocles

Ahl, Frederick. *Sophocles' Oedipus: Evidence and Self-Conviction*. 1991.
Bates, William Nickerson. *Sophocles: Poet and Dramatist*. 1961.
Bloom, Harold, ed. *Sophocles. Modern Critical Views*. 1990.
Bowra, C. M. *Sophoclean Tragedy*. 1944.
Ehrenberg, Victor. *Sophocles and Pericles*. 1954.
Ferguson, Francis. *"Oedipus*: Ritual and Play." *The Idea of a Theatre*. 1949.
Freud, Sigmund. *"Oedipus Rex." The Interpretation of Dreams*. 1900.
Gellie, G. H. *Sophocles: A Reading*. 1972.
Greengard, Carola. *Theatre in Crisis: Sophocles' Reconstruction of Genre and Politics in "Philoctetes."* 1987.
Kirkwood, Gordon M. *A Study of Sophoclean Drama*. 1958.
Kiso, Akiko. *The Lost Sophocles*. 1984.
Kitto, H. D. F. *Sophocles: Dramatist and Philosopher*. 1958.
Knox, Bernard M.W. *The Heroic Temper: Studies in Sophoclean Tragedy*. 1964.
Mandel, Oscar, ed. *Philoctetes and the Fall of Troy: Plays, Documents, Iconography, Interpretations*. 1981.
O'Brien, Michael J., ed. *Twentieth Century Interpretations of Oedipus Rex*. 1968.
Segal, Charles. *Oedipus Tyrannus: Tragic Heroism and the Limits of Knowledge*. 1993.
_____. *Sophocles' Tragic World: Divinity, Nature, Society*. 1995.
_____. *Tragedy and Civilization: An Interpretation of Sophocles*. 1982.
Steiner, George, *Antigones*. 1984.
Velacott, Philip. *Sophocles and Oedipus*. 1971.
Waldock, A. J. A. *Sophocles the Dramatist*. 1951.
Webster, T. B. L. *An Introduction to Sophocles*. 1936. Rpt. 1969.
Whitman, Cedric H. *The Heroic Paradox: Essays on Homer, Sophocles and Aristophanes*. 1982.
_____. *Sophocles: A Study in Heroic Humanism*. 1951.
Wilson, Edmund. *"Philoctetes*: The Wound and the Bow." *The Wound and the Bow*. 1965.
Wilson, Joseph P. *The Hero and the City: An Interpretation of Sophocles' Oedipus at Colonus*. 1997.
Winnington-Ingram, R. P. *Sophocles: An Interpretation*. 1980.
Woodard, Thomas, ed. *Sophocles: A Collection of Critical Essays*. 1966.

Sophocles: Recommended Translations and Commentaries

Berg, Stephen, and Diskin Clay, trans. *Oedipus the King*. 1978.
Brown, Andrew L., trans. and comm. *Antigone*. 1988.
Fitzgerald, Robert, trans. *Oedipus at Colonus*. 1954.
Grene, David, trans. *Electra*. 1957.
_____, trans. *Oedipus the King*. 1954.
_____, trans. *Philoctetes*. 1957.
Jameson, Michael, trans. *The Women of Trachis*. 1957.

Jebb, R. C., ed. and comm. *Sophocles: The Plays and Fragments*. 7 vols. 1883–1914.
Lloyd-Jones, Hugh, ed. and trans. *Sophocles*. 2 vols. 1992–1994.
_____, ed. and trans. *Sophocles: Fragments*. 1996.
Moore, John., trans. *Ajax*. 1957.
Parry, Adam M., trans. and comm. *Ajax*. 1970.
Pound, Ezra, trans. *Sophokles' Elektra*. 1987.
_____, trans. *Women of Trachis*. 1957.
Ussher, R. G., trans. and comm. *Philoctetes*. 1990.
Williams, C. K., and Gregory Dickerson, trans. *Women of Trachis*. 1978.
Yeats, William Butler, trans. *King Oedipus*. 1928.
_____, trans. *Oedipus at Colonus*. 1932.

Critical Studies of Euripides
Appleton, Reginald B. *Euripides the Idealist*. 1927.
Barlow, Shirley A. *The Imagery of Euripides*. 2nd ed. 1986.
Bates, Walter Nickerson. *Euripides: A Student of Human Nature*. 1930.
Burian, Peter, ed. *New Directions in Euripidean Criticism*. 1985.
Burnett, Anne Pippin. *Catastrophe Survived: Euripides' Plays of Mixed Reversal*. 1971.
Conacher, D. J. *Euripidean Drama: Myth, Theme and Structure*. 1967.
Decharme, Paul. *Euripides and the Spirit of His Times*. 1906.
Dunn, Francis M. *Tragedy's End: Closure and Innovation in Euripidean Drama*. 1996.
Foley, Helene P. *Ritual Irony: Poetry and Sacrifice in Euripides*. 1985.
Greenwood, L. H. *Aspects of Euripidean Tragedy*. 1953.
Gregory, Justina. *Euripides and the Instruction of the Athenians*. 1991.
Grube, G. M. A. *The Drama of Euripides*. 1941. Rpt. 1961.
McDermott, Emily. *Euripides' "Medea": The Incarnation of Disorder*. 1989.
Michelini, A.N. *Euripides and the Tragic Tradition*. 1987.
Murray, Gilbert. *Euripides and His Age*. 1922. Rpt. 1946.
Norwood, Gilbert. *Essays on Euripidean Drama*. 1954.
Powell, Anton, ed. *Euripides, Women and Sexuality*. 1990.
Pucci, Pietro. *The Violence of Pity in Euripides' Medea*. 1980.
Rabinowitz, Nancy Sorkin. *Anxiety Veiled: Euripides and the Traffic in Women*. 1993.
Segal, Charles. *Dionysian Poetics and Euripides' Bacchae*. 1982.
_____. *Euripides and the Poetics of Sorrow*. 1993.
Segal, Erich, ed. *Euripides: A Collection of Critical Essays*. 1968.
Velacott, Philip. *Ironic Drama: A Study of Euripides' Method and Meaning*. 1975.
Verall, A. W. *Euripides the Rationalist*. 1895.
Webster, T. B. L. *The Tragedies of Euripides*. 1967.
Whitman, Cedric H. *Euripides and the Full Circle of Myth*. 1974.
Winnington-Ingram, R. P. *Euripides and Dionysus*. 1948.

Euripides: Recommended Translations and Commentaries
Arrowsmith, William, trans. and comm. *Alcestis*. 1974.
_____, trans. *The Bacchae*. 1959.

_____, trans. *Hecuba*. 1958.
_____, trans. *Orestes*. 1958.
Bagg, Robert, trans. and comm. *The Bakkhai*. 1978.
_____, trans. and comm. *Hippolytos*. 1973.
Barlow, Shirley A., trans. and comm. *Trojan Women*. 1986.
Braun, Richard Emil, trans. *Rhesos*. 1978.
Burian, Peter, and Brian Swann, trans. *The Phoenician Women*. 1981.
Collard, Christopher, trans. and comm. *Hecuba*. 1991.
_____, and others, eds., trans. and comm. *Euripides: Selected Fragmentary Plays*. Vol. I. 1995.
Conacher, Desmond J., trans. and comm. *Alcestis*. 1988.
Craik, Elizabeth, trans. and comm. *Phoenician Women*. 1988.
Cropp, M. J., trans. and comm. *Electra*. 1988.
Di Piero, W. S., trans. *Ion*. Comm. Peter Burian. 1996.
Ferguson, John. *Euripides' Medea and Electra: A Companion to the Penguin Translation*. 1987.
Grene, David, trans. *Hippolytus*. 1955.
Halleran, Michael R., trans. and comm. *The Heracles of Euripides*. Rev. ed. 1992.
Kirk, G. S., trans. and comm. *The Bacchae*. 1970. Rpt. 1979.
Knox, Bernard M. W., trans. and comm. *Medea*. 1970.
Lattimore, Richmond, trans. *Alcestis*. 1955.
_____, trans. *Helen*. 1956.
_____, trans. *Iphigeneia in Tauris*. 1973.
_____, trans. *Trojan Women*. 1959.
Lembke, Janet, and Kenneth J. Reckford, trans. *Hecuba*. 1991.
Lloyd, Michael, trans. and comm. *Andromache*. 1994.
Merwin, W. S., and George E. Dimock, Jr., trans. *Iphigeneia at Aulis*. 1978.
Michie, James, and Colin Leach, trans. *Helen*. 1981.
Page, Denys L., ed. and comm. *Euripides' Medea*. 1938. Rpt. 1976.
Peck, John, and Frank Nisetich, trans. *Orestes*. 1995.
Podlecki, A. J., trans. and comm. *Euripides' Medea*. 1991.
Taylor, Henry, and Robert A. Brooks, trans. *The Children of Herakles*. 1981.
Walker, Charles R., trans. *Iphigenia in Aulis*. 1958.
Warner, Rex, trans. *Medea*. 1955.
Warren, Rosanna, and Stephen Scully, trans. *Suppliant Women*. 1995.
West, M. L., trans. and comm. *Orestes*. 1987.

Index

Acheron 80
Achilles 20, 103, 105, 108, 115, 131, 132, 133
Acropolis 113
adelphē 20
Admetus 92–96, 98, 106
Aegeus 71, 103
Aegisthus 23, 60, 63, 66
Aegospotomi 137
Aeschines 21, 30
Aeschylus 1, 3, 12, 13, 20, 23, 25, 33, 45–56, 59–72, 83, 87, 88, 99, 100, 101, 108, 113, 120, 124, 126, 128, 132, 135, 137; *Agamemnon* 22, 40, 45–46, 59–66, 111–12; *Cretan Women* 20; *Danaid* trilogy 47–50, 55; *Daughters of Danaos* 55; *Egyptians* 55; *Eumenides* 12, 17–18, 25, 64, 68–70, 72; *Libation Bearers* 66–68; *Myrmidons* 20; *Oedipodeia* 46; *Oresteia* 46, 47, 48, 49, 55, 59–72, 79, 98, 120, 137; *Persians* 9, 45; *Philoctetes* 113; *Prometheia* 49; *Prometheus Bound* 48, 49; *Seven Against Thebes* 12, 46, 47, 59, 73, 79; *Suppliant Maidens* 12, 33, 45–56
Africa 50
Agamemnon 40, 45, 60, 63–64, 65, 66, 105, 131, 132, 134
agōn 29, 60, 131
agora 8
aischrologia 34
Ajax 13, 22–23, 29, 103, 105
Alcestis 22, 87–96, 133
Alcibiades 37, 111
Amazonomachia 24
Amazons 24, 53, 54, 71
amazos 24
anagnorisis 29, 94, 126

Anaxagoras 88
andreia 91, 92
Andromache 99
anēr 19, 92
anorexia 23, 79
anthrōpos 19,
antidemocrats 37, 112, 128
Antigone 13, 22, 39, 74–84
Aphrodite 55, 136
Apollo 7, 64, 68, 69–70, 78, 98, 128, 130
Areopagus 70–71
Ares 71
aretē 91, 114, 115, 120, 132
Argive 53
Argos 48, 54, 55, 128, 129
aristocracy 5, 73
Aristophanes 14, 15, 33, 99, 100–101; *Frogs* 15, 87, 97, 131; *Thesmophoriazusai* 33, 99, 100–101
Aristophanes of Byzantium 89, 127
aristos 19
Aristotle 3, 20, 22, 28, 31, 88, 91, 103; *Nichomachean Ethics* 22; *Poetics* 92; *Politics* 28, 31, 91
arrēn 19
Artemis 45, 61, 72, 134
Asclepius 121
Athena 25, 26, 61, 65, 70, 79, 116
Athenaeus 117
Athēnaios 21
Atreïdae 118, 119, 120
Atreus 46, 59, 61, 64, 129, 134
Attic Greek 19
Attica 6–7, 54, 71, 112, 113

barbarian 64, 76, 101, 106
Beckett, Samuel: *Waiting for Godot* 114
bia 49
blood-kinship 68, 69

INDEX

boulē 8, 71

Cassandra 22, 59, 63, 64
catharsis 39
Charon 90
chastity 51, 55, 126
Chekhov, Anton: *The Cherry Orchard* 90
Choerilus 41
chorēgos 9
chorus 4, 6, 12–13, 14, 17, 38, 40, 47, 62, 66, 67, 68, 79, 81, 83, 89, 92, 94, 114, 123, 136
Chrysothemis 75
chthonic deities 59, 77
citizenship 27, 28, 113
citizenship law 26–28
City Dionysia 2, 4, 8, 14, 34–38, 41, 84, 113, 127, 131
civil disobedience 14, 15, 74, 124
Cleisthenes 5, 10, 27
Cleon 5
Clytemnestra 22, 40, 55, 60, 62–67, 70, 75, 102, 111, 125, 129, 130, 131, 132
Committee for Public Safety 112
constitution 4, 23
Corinthians 106
coup d'état 15, 112, 124
Creon 29, 40, 74–84
Crete 68

damar 20
Danaians 48
Danaos 33, 48, 50, 51, 53, 54–55
Danton 10
death squads 112
Deceleia 112
Deianara 39, 91
Delian League 35, 42
Demeter 7, 55
dēmoi 21, 73
dēmos 5, 8, 28
Demosthenes 17, 21, 79

deus ex machina 104, 114, 120, 121, 131
didaskalos 13
Didymus 106
dikaiosunē 91
dikē 83
Diodorus of Sicily 24
Dionysian 7, 8, 38
Dionysus 6–7, 8, 26, 41, 70, 134, 135, 136
diptych 76
dithyramb 48
domos 90, 95
dramaturgy 46, 47, 59, 62, 82, 101

Egypt 48, 50, 56, 125, 127
Egyptians 48, 50, 51, 55
Egyptos 48, 51
ekklēsia 8, 71
Electra 67, 128, 129, 130
Eleusinian Mysteries 37
Eleusis 7
eleutheria 115
Epaphos 48–49
ephebe 38, 43, 102, 115
Ephialtes 5, 71
erastēs 20
Erichthonius 25
eromenos 20
eros 80, 111, 112
Eteocles 40, 46, 59, 73
Euripides 1, 3, 12, 13, 14, 20, 33, 54, 82, 87–96, 99–109, 113, 116, 118, 123–138; *Alcestis* 89–96, 102, 104; *Bakkhai* 124, 131, 134, 135–37: *Chrysippus* 20; *Cretans* 20; *Electra* 88, 137; *Hecuba* 22, 100; *Helen* 87, 124–127; *Hippolytus* 26, 137; *Iphigeneia at Aulis* 124, 131–135, 137; *Medea* 26, 95, 100–9, 113; *Orestes* 89, 111, 123, 124, 127–31; *Philoctetes* 111, 113; *Trojan Women* 100, 123, 125
Eurydice 82

female masks 41, 70
femaleness 23, 47, 53, 100
feminine 9, 20–21, 25, 29, 38, 127, 132
feminist 13, 33, 50, 75, 100
feminized 7, 39
fertility 6, 34, 35, 36, 136
festivals 4, 8, 14, 15, 33, 34, 35, 41, 42
first prize 84, 87
French Academy 9
funerals 74, 91
Furies 24, 68–70, 78

Gaia 55, 68
Gela 72
gender *hubris* 29, 70, 78, 92, 100
gender ideology 1, 7, 19, 22, 23, 47, 53, 65, 67, 77, 79, 80, 104, 128, 133, 135
genē 73
genitalia 34
genitals 34
genos gunaikōn 19
gods 36, 59, 71, 128
Gorgons 24
government of the Five Thousand 113
gunē 20, 23, 66, 78, 95
Gymnopaideia 34

Hades 81
Haemon 78, 82
hamartia 78, 79, 94, 103
Hamlet 93
Harpies 24
Hector 99
Hecuba 22
Hedda Gabler 102, 103
Hegel 74, 76
Helen 40, 64, 65, 87, 123, 125–127, 129–130, 131, 133, 134
Helios 104
Hellespont 45
Henry, Patrick 10
Hephaestus 25

Hera 48, 106
Herakles 23, 45, 89, 95, 96, 98, 113, 115–116, 119, 120, 121
Hermes 33, 36
Hermione 95, 129, 130
herms 36
Herodotus 33, 36, 50, 123, 124
heroic code 108, 114, 115
Hesiod 18–19; *Works and Days* 18–19
hetaira 17, 20
heterosexuality 20
Hippocrates 79
Hippolytus 26, 40, 136
Homer: *Iliad* 99, 108, 115; *Odyssey* 116
homosexuality 20
hoplite 4, 113
hubris 22, 29, 45, 50, 51, 53, 60, 70, 77, 78, 79, 82, 84, 92, 100
hustera 23
hymn to *Eros* 39, 80, 111
hyperfeminine 2, 38, 39
Hypermestra 48, 55
hysteria 23, 79

Ibsen, Henrik 87, 103, 120; *A Doll House* 105; *Hedda Gabler* 102–3; *Little Eyolf* 120
Io 46, 48, 56
Iphigeneia 40, 66, 91, 131, 132, 133, 134
Ireland 74
Ismene 22, 75, 78, 81
Italian *commedia* 38

Jason 26, 40, 101, 103, 104–9

kleos 91
Kreon 106
Kronos 69

Laius 46
law court 21, 71
Lemnos 114, 121
Lenaea 41

Lenin 10
Lesbos 18
lex talionis 68
Life of Aeschylus 17–18, 72
Life of Euripides 87
Lynceus 55

Macedonia 87, 131, 137
maenads 7
male-bonding 2, 29, 34–35, 96
maleness 2, 34, 41, 47, 100, 136
Manifesto of the Communist Party 10
Marathon 61, 118
marriage 28, 47, 50, 51, 56, 69, 78, 80, 90, 93, 96, 127, 130
Marx 10
masculine 1, 7, 20, 25, 26, 29, 35, 36, 38, 41, 47, 55, 61, 76, 77, 79, 91, 94, 100, 101, 102, 103, 117, 127, 132, 133, 134
masculinity 37, 127, 137
matricide 59, 66, 67
matrilinear 7, 68, 69
Medea 1, 22, 40, 100–9
Melian dialogue 128
Menelaus 123, 125, 126, 127, 128, 131, 134
mātēr 20
metics 5, 27
military 4, 8, 15, 37
Minoan 7, 25, 68
misogyny 29, 78, 84, 100
Mnesilochus 33, 99
monody 98
myth 11, 12, 14, 26, 47, 106, 113, 135, 138

Neoptolemus 114–120
new comedy 138
nomina 83
Nora 105
numphos 20

Odysseus 29, 113, 115–121, 132

Oedipus 79, 103, 115
oikos 27, 73, 90
old comedy 34, 138
oligarchy 5, 6, 11, 59, 73
oligarchy of the Four Hundred 112–113
Olympic games 34
Olympus 26, 89, 118
omophagia 136
orchestra 6, 13, 37
Orestes 40, 61, 65, 66, 67, 105, 127, 128, 129, 130

Paine, Thomas 10
Palestine 74
pallaka 17, 20
Pandora 19
Paris 125
Parthenon 24
parthenos 20
patēr 66
patriarch 27, 55, 59, 63, 64, 66, 67, 68, 77
patriarchy 1, 23, 26, 27, 36, 38, 41, 47, 50, 53, 54, 56, 59, 62, 67, 68, 69, 71, 77, 83, 84, 87, 90, 92, 99, 100, 101, 104, 106, 108, 124, 130, 136
Patroclus 20
Pausanias 105
Peisistratus 4, 6, 7
peithō 50, 119
Pelasgos 45, 48, 53, 54, 55, 56
Peloponnesian War 5, 14, 15, 37, 88, 102, 111, 119, 124, 125
Peloponnesus 112
Pentheus 29, 135, 136, 137
peripeteia 94, 123, 124, 126, 133, 135
Pericles 4–5, 9, 24, 26, 71, 74, 84, 87, 91
Persians 45
Phaedra 40, 137
phallophoroi 35
phallus 35, 36, 41, 42; phalluses 7, 37, 40
Pheres 92, 93, 98
Philoctetes 113–122

INDEX

phratrē 28, 73; *phratrai* 21
Phrynichus 6, 9, 14, 41; *Phoenicians* 9; *Sack of Miletus* 9, 14
Pindar 106
Plato 10
Plutarch 36, 127
Pnyx 33
polis 8, 10, 11, 12, 14, 25, 26, 28, 47, 50, 54, 59, 68, 71, 73, 74, 76, 79, 83, 99, 100, 104, 107, 109, 114, 118, 119, 120, 121, 126, 127, 130, 136, 137
politēs 21
Polyneices 74, 79
Polyxena 91
pompē 35
pornē 20
Priam 117
proboulos 112
Procne 76
Prometheus 118
propaganda 6, 8, 9, 133
Prospero 115
protagonist 12, 13, 39, 63, 82, 89, 103, 104
Protagoras 88, 89, 95; *Contradictions* 89; *On the Gods* 88
proxenoi 6
Pylades 128
Pyrrhus 117
Pythagoras 5

rape 20, 51
regicide 67
religion 11, 17, 68, 69, 88, 127, 136
revolution 10, 15, 38, 124
Rights of Man 10
ritual 2, 7, 8, 9, 11, 17, 18, 29, 33, 34, 35, 38, 41, 96, 134, 135
Romeo and Juliet 105
Rural Dionysia 7, 34, 35, 41

Salamis 123
Samos 112

Sappho 18
satyr play 41, 89
scholiast 89, 105
Scott, Clement 105
Scribe, Eugene 9
Scylla and Charybdis 24
second actor 54
Semele 136
Seven Days in May 59
sex 20–21, 52, 80, 91
sexual 20, 23, 26, 29, 35, 40, 47, 64, 80, 117, 126
sexuality 17, 18, 19, 34, 53–54, 56, 126, 127, 129, 130, 135, 137
Shakespeare, William 12, 40, 50, 117; *Antony and Cleopatra* 50; *Hamlet* 117; *The Tempest* 115; *The Winter's Tale* 95
Shelley, Percy Bysshe 1
Sicilian expedition 37, 87, 111, 112, 124, 125
Sicily 112, 125
Sirens 24
Socrates 127
sophists 88
Sophocles 1, 3, 13, 50, 73–84, 88, 89, 99, 100, 101, 108, 112–121, 135, 137; *Ajax* 22–23, 76, 116; *Antigone* 22, 39, 40, 73–84, 89, 111; *Electra* 75; *Lovers of Achilles* 20; *Oedipus at Colonus* 50, 115; *Philoctetes* 21, 113–21, 135; *Tereus* 75–76; *Women of Trachis* 23, 39–40, 45, 76, 116
sophrosunē 91, 115
sparagmos 136
Sparta 5–6, 20, 28, 34
State and Revolution 10
Stesichorus 125
stichomythia 60
Stone, Oliver 59; *JFK* 59
stratēgos 84
Strindberg 27
superplot 46, 47, 48, 59

supertext 46
Suppliant Maidens 45–56, 75
Syracuse 111

terrorism 124
terrorists 128, 129, 130
Theatre of Dionysus 4, 5, 38, 70, 127
thēlē 19
Themistocles 5, 9, 26
Theoclymenus 126, 127
theology 6, 49, 68, 69
Theonoë 126–127
Theoric Fund 5
Thermodon River 24
Theseus 24, 71, 137
Thesmophoria 33–34, 41, 56
Thesmophorion 33
Thespis 7, 41; *Games of Pelias* 41; *Pentheus* 41; *Youths* 41
thiasos 7
third actor 121
Thirty Tyrants 137
Three Days of the Condor 59
three-actor play 95, 96
threnos 82
Thucydides 3, 10, 37, 111, 112, 113, 124, 129
thugatēr 20
thumelē 37
Timarkhos 21
Tiresias 82, 83
tragic dilemma 55
transvestite 2, 7, 18, 38–39, 41
trireme 4
Trojan War 59, 64, 65, 118, 125, 131
trope of impossibility 126, 133
Trotsky 10
Troy 45, 61, 62, 65, 66, 117, 121, 125, 127
two-actor play 95
tyranny 6, 11, 71, 74, 83
tyrant 4, 54, 60, 79

victim 22, 40, 75, 90, 91, 101, 104, 106, 108
victimization 39, 40, 75
violence 23, 67
vir 19
virtus 19

wedding 28, 55, 80
wife 19, 20, 27, 79, 90, 95, 96, 104, 108, 126
wife/woman 19, 20, 23, 66, 90, 91, 92, 94, 95, 96, 103

xenios 49
Xenophon 23
Xerxes 45

Zeus 26, 48, 49, 51, 52, 55, 56, 64, 65, 66, 68, 69, 70